FOUR SECTIONS
40 PAGES
Thursday Afternoon
June 9, 1949
Vol. 54 • Price 5 Cents

al

CRASH

R

MW00768766

...der Recoverin...

...for
...pla
...For
base recently, ...to 1
cover fully, it was announc...
yesterday.

His physician at the base h...
...as p...
...l m...
...a g...
...treat
...sion
...to 1

...ight Chance
...or Pilot Here

...pt. James L. Louden, 28, of
...est Garden Rd., Brentwood,
...given only slight chance of
...very today from injuries he

...ESTERN
UNION
1191
JOSEPH L. EGAN
PRESIDENT

SYMBOLS
DL=Day Letter
NL=Night Letter
LC=Deferred Cable
NLT=Cable Night Letter
Ship Radiogram

...tern is STANDARD TIME at point of origin. Time of receipt is STANDARD TIME at point of destination

...PD

... WUX FORT GEORGE G MEADE JUNE 9 1949 457PM

...APTAIN JAMES L LOUDEN IS SERIOUSLY ILL STATION HOSPITAL
... TO AIRPLANE CRASH NINTH OF JUNE 1949 PD RECOMMEND
...ANDING OFFICER BARKSDALE AIRBASE SHREVEPORT LOUSIANA

...PPRECIATE SUGGESTIONS FROM ITS PATRONS CONCERNING ITS SERVICE

...rash Survivor
...ay Be Moved

...apt. James Louden, public in-
...mation officer of the 47th bomb
...g, may be removed to a genera
...pital for treatment for injuries
...eived in the crash of a B-45 jet
...mber near Barksdale Air Force
...se two weeks ago.
...he base public information
...ice said yesterday that Captain
...uden is still in a critical condi-
...n, but is scheduled to be re-
...ved to a general hospital "as
...n as officers orders authorizing
... move are received."

Plucky Jim— Sept 15/19

Capt. JAMES L. LOUDE...
who narrowly escaped dea...
when a B-45 jet bomber crash...
two months ago, was back...
Barksdale air force base th...
week on a visit.

The crash cost the lives...
two other fliers, Capts. RALF...
L. SMITH, 315 Ratcliff stre...
and MILTON O. COSTELLO,...
Chicago. The accident occurr...
as the plane was on its dow...
wind leg of a touch-and-go lar...

In addition to our 80+ years of age, "Big Jim" and I have other special bonds based on our mutual love of baseball, our exceptional wives, God and our great country. I loved "On God's Wings" and its inspiring messages and want to thank Teri for honoring not only her dad, but our generation as well.

— **Joe DiGangi,** Bull Pen Catcher for the New York Yankees, 1933; Navy Seabee, WWII-Pacific

My father, who flew one of the first B-45's, found it to be an aircraft of great promise. However, he knew there would be accidents. Teri Louden, from her uniquely personal perspective, has now told of the most harrowing and miraculous of these accidents. There was nothing left of the aircraft, nothing left of two men... and the third, Jim Louden, had to be found and pieced back together.

— **Patricia Chapman Meder,** daughter of Brigadier General Willis F. Chapman, USAF (commander of the 47th bomb group where the B-45 was introduced), and wife Charlotte

"On God's Wings" beautifully captures the wonderful life lessons and spiritual gifts that "Big Jim" and his daughter have shared with those of us who have been fortunate enough to have known them over the years. There is a great word for the two of them... firecrackers!!

— **David Hanke,** Senior Vice President, McKesson Corporation

"Teri Louden's book reveals the values instilled in children from growing up in a military family: integrity, perseverance, a sense of adventure, and the inspiration and confidence to pursue their own dreams."

— **Linda A. Burns,** daughter of pilot Lt. Colonel Joseph Burns, US Air Force (Ret.)

"Big Jim" was always a larger than life kind of guy, and Teri captures that so perfectly. However, the extra special part of "On God's Wings" is the testimony given to the strength of character required to be the supportive military wife — like her dear mother and my very good friend Peggy Louden.

> — **Marge Kaufmann,** Air Force pilot wife and supportive friend of Peggy Louden after "Big Jim's" crash

What a joy it has been to have Jim Louden as part of our faith community. In fact, I've given the "Hubba Dubba Man" a new nickname. I call him "Joyful Jim." Since his move here several years ago, his faith, optimism, generosity and love of Christ have touched many lives. "On God's Wing's" is a wonderful tribute to this man of faith. I can honestly say that Jim lives what he believes.

> — **Reverend Charles M. Zimmerman,** Senior Pastor, First Lutheran Church, Greensboro, NC.

Jim Louden's will to live was, I believe, very much driven by his wanting to fly again— Teri has so perfectly captured his miracle story and the highs and lows of life in the military. A wonderful tribute to military men and families who have sacrificed so much for the love of their country.

> — **Pat Roberts Coleman,** Air Force pilot wife and supportive friend of Peggy Louden after "Big Jim's" crash

Jim is a very kind and compassionate individual who loves life and lives it in a full and Christian way. He is easy to meet, easy to love, and if you mind your manners, and ask him nicely, he may just serenade you with a little tune on his harmonica.

> — **E. Faison Williams,** Secretary of Creasy Proctor Masonic Lodge 679, Fayetteville, NC

Believe in miracles. They happen every day.

Wishing You

Many Blessings '0

Teri Louden

ON GOD'S WINGS

TERI LOUDEN

A daughter's inspirational story of her dad and his miracle.

THE LOUDEN NETWORK, INC.

CORONADO, CA

www.ongodswings.com
1 (800) 214-6811

$\mathcal{A}$ portion of the *On God's Wings* profits are donated to various non-for-profit organizations.

Published by

The Louden Network, Inc.
1125 Loma Avenue, #109
Coronado, CA 92118
I (800) 214-6811

www.ongodswings.com
info@ongodswings.com

ISBN: 0-9753926-0-3

DEDICATION

*To my mother who gave me my roots
and my dad who gave me my wings.*

TABLE OF CONTENTS

ACKNOWLEDGEMENTS

I sat down with my dad to write this special tribute on June 6, 2004, a very special day indeed. Sixty years ago on this same date, my father flew two missions in the Normandy beachhead area of France, and along with thousands of other men and women, made D-Day an unforgettable day in history. In addition to the special individuals who helped make this book a reality, we would be remiss if we did not thank the many men and women who have sacrificed their time and their lives to keep the freedoms of our great country.

My dad and I will forever be grateful for the many wonderful individuals that provided different, but equally valuable support for making this book possible. We thank each and every one of them for contributing to this story and helping to spread the message about the wonders of living *On God's Wings.*

My beloved mother— for leaving behind the many detailed scrapbooks and photo albums filled with photos, telegrams, newspaper clippings, and documentation about the realities of my dad's B-45 crash and our military traveling life. And, for providing the all-important "roots" to balance our traveling and adventure-filled military life.

Ned Touchstone— for finding my dad and saving his life that fateful day of the crash on June 9, 1949.

Pat Roberts Coleman and Marge Kaufmann— for being there to comfort and support my mother following my dad's devastating crash and subsequent early days of recuperation.

Jim Sharpe— who was in my dad's 47th Bomb Group, present on the field the day of my dad's crash and provided invaluable information and contacts for me in writing this book.

ACKNOWLEDGEMENTS

Ted Jakubowski— for taking the time and initiative to research and eventually find Ned Touchstone, the living angel who played a critical role in my dad's miracle survival at the scene of his crash.

Larry Cheek— the writer for the Fayetteville Observer newspaper who documented Ted Jakubowski's story that was published in the Fayetteville Observer and subsequently produced as an article entitled "The T-Shirt" in the book called *The Legacy of Daedalus, War Stories and Flying Tales,* published in the year 2000 by the Order of Daedalians.[1]

Patricia Chapman Meder— who is another proud military daughter like myself and provided insights, information, and photos about her father, Brigadier General Willis Chapman, USAF. He was the proud commander of the first jet bomber group in the US Air Force, the 47th Bomb Group, and also my dad's mentor. I would like to extend a special thank you to him and his wife, Charlotte, who provided such valuable support and love for my mom and dad in the critical days after the crash and the years beyond.

Robert Cardenas, Retired USAF Brigadier General and the Chief US Air Force Test Pilot for the XB-45 at Muroc Lake, California (now Edwards Air Force Base)— a remarkable man who also has amazing miracle survival stories of his own, Bob shared incredible history and photos from his test pilot years and experience with the early B-45 jet bombers.

Maj. Walter E. Collier (Ret.) USAF—who sent me his incredible compilation of facts, statistics, and information on the B-45, our nation's first jet bomber, and introduced me to Retired USAF Col. Eric Linhof who, along with Walter, flew B-45s in the 1950s when the 47th Bomb Group was stationed in RAF Station Sculthorpe, England. Thanks to both of them for providing me with the history of the last years of flight for the B-45.

John Fredericksen, Ph.D.— special thanks to this aviation historian for providing his review of the technical appendix about the B-45 Tornado. He has been researching the B-45 for some time now and has plans to

---

[1] *An international association of pilots that was founded in 1934 to honor WWI pilots, the first pilots to serve in war. The last Daedalian that flew in WWI passed away in the year 2003 at the age of 104.

write a book about the history of this plane, our nation's first operational jet bomber.

Jennifer Willis— my dedicated business associate who was my friend and support base at the time of my injury in Chicago, and as I recuperated, helped make my move to Coronado, California, possible, and spurred me on to take the time to write "Big Jim's" story.

Meg Cox—my long-time friend and author extraordinaire who provided many words of wisdom to me during the concept stage of *On God's Wings* as well as during my book-writing process. Meg lectures about family rituals and has recently published a wonderful book on this topic: *The Book of New Family Traditions: How to Create Great Rituals for Holidays & Everyday*.

All of my friends and colleagues from CardioNet— for providing me constant support and confidence when I was part of the senior management launch team and for their respect for my dad and for my passion and desire to spend focused time to write his story. A special thanks to Jim Sweeney, the CEO of CardioNet, for his belief in me, and to Larry Watts, the VP of Marketing, who kept my enthusiasm burning as he continuously convinced me that, yes, I could indeed write and publish this book.

Chuck Lauer, Corporate Vice President, Crain Communications, Inc. and publisher *Modern Healthcare*— for being so supportive during the early years as I launched The Louden Network, Inc. and his continued encouragement, mentoring, and friendship over the years. He also inspired me with his two books: *Soar With The Eagles* and *Reach For The Stars*.

Peg Ford— who helped me begin turning my thoughts and ideas about my story into reality by conducting invaluable investigative research, documenting my thoughts and those of my dad, and meeting with me every week for months on end to keep the book alive while I was working full-time. Thanks also to my friends at Café Madrid, Café 1134, and Tent City Restaurant on Coronado Island for providing Peg and me with the perfect venues for our weekly meetings!

$\mathcal{A}$CKNOWLEDGEMENTS

Dan Poynter—author of *The Self-Publishing Manual* and self-publishing expert who helped guide me early on as I learned from his books, educational retreats, and workshops.

Michael Lovett, President/CEO and Ron Powers, Director, Merchandise at Ingram Book Group, Inc.— for taking the time to personally meet with me and my dad at their headquarters in Nashville and providing invaluable advice, contacts, and service support.

My brother, Jim Louden, Jr.— for providing his perspective on being the son of "Big Jim" and for being a great older brother.

Brenda Wing— for providing her wonderful friendship ever since our college years, and to her and her great husband Dick for their never-ending support and encouragement for me and my dad.

Jean Pierre and Linda Marques— for their special attention during my injury as I learned how therapeutic yoga and relaxation would enhance my healing. We grew together, as they had just launched their Coronado Yoga and Wellness Center when I moved to Coronado.

My many special friends— who supported my efforts by listening, providing ideas and encouragement, and never growing weary of my never-ending updates on the book progress. And... for always extending their love and respect for my dad. I will forever be grateful. I couldn't have done it without you!

The Nashville Fan Club—Jim Gilmore who graciously provided his Nashville studio, Audio Productions, and his superior music-recording talents to record the *On God's Wings* CD with me and my dad; Colin Parker who assisted him that day and Jim's wife, Janet Schreibman, a dear friend; Rip Williams, for playing his guitar with my dad for the CD and to both him and his wife, Amy, for their years of love, friendship, and prayers; The friends from my years in Nashville who showed up for the "Big Jim Fan Club" dinner to celebrate the release of the *On God's Wings* book and CD.

The *On God's Wings* **launch team**— for their talents, time and dedication, creative ideas, continued encouragement, and never-ending belief and enthusiasm for this book.

As they say, "It Takes a Team!"

Jeniffer Thompson— project director extraordinaire and an incredible cheerleader and champion, staying always positive in the face of monumental deadlines and details.

Kris Grant— content editor, unbelievable creative word genius, and public relations guru—also master multi-tasker as she edited this book while launching her own ventures.

Cathy Kessler— copy editor who dotted our i's, crossed our t's, and recommended all the special finishing touches.

McNulty Creative— Mary McNulty for her help envisioning what would make the perfect book cover and Jack Gatlin for his amazing design skills, which he used to turn the book cover and layout design vision into a reality. Coincidently, what fun to work with another fellow North Carolina State University alumnus who also ended up on the other side of the country in San Diego.

Future-Ink— Christianna Connell and Jeuné Ortiz for implementing their great programming and design skills in creating the *On God's Wings'* website.

Penny Sansevieri— awesome marketing and author promotion services expert who provided the expertise, guidance, and confidence for me to believe that I could self-publish this book and reach the many audiences that would appreciate and enjoy the story.

Monica Neville— who came to me just in the knick of time to provide valuable insight and moral support.

And, of course, we thank THE GOOD LORD, the number one reason for this book and for everything in our lives! AMEN.

FOREWORD

My dad told me war was h-e-l-l and that there are no atheists in cockpits or foxholes — I believe he was right, and if you've ever been there, you may feel the same way.

I've seen war, and by the grace of God, I've lived to tell. I am a blessed man. I've flown in four wars, and I've watched many good men die for the freedom that this great country enjoys. I am proud to be an American. I cherish my freedom to be a Christian and to say what I feel is truth. I will say unto anyone who will listen: "Do unto others, as you would have them do unto you." For if you can be nice to all people and truly love them, and maintain a positive attitude — you can live without fear or worry and enjoy your time on earth.

It is with great honor that I thank my daughter, Teri, who has written this book about my life, my family, and the many blessings that we have enjoyed. I am hopeful that within these pages you might find something that touches you, something that speaks to you and gives you the courage to slow down and recognize your own gifts and the gifts of your parents and mentors. Life is a blessing. Every man, woman, and child is a miracle. We each have a story.

Take the time to hear the stories of your elders. Share your stories with your children, your sons, and your daughters alike. Fathers, nurture your children, encourage them to follow their aspirations. Trust that if you shower your children with love and interest they will grow strong with confidence and have the strength to trust their gifts and be the best they can be in the best country in the world — the United States of America.

Jim Louden

Lt. Col. Jim Louden, US Air Force (Ret.)

PREFACE

*"Yesterday's a cancelled check, tomorrow's a promissory note,
and every day begins a new chapter."*

— Jim Louden

I was 45-years-old when I came to know my father. Oh, he had always
been there, a devoted dad, nurturer, and provider. He and my mother
had gifted my brother and me with love and values. But it wasn't
until I encountered chronic, agonizing pain that I was able to receive
the blessings of his inner strength. That strength, rooted in a deep
Christian faith, is what allowed my father to survive a crash in the
first United States jet bomber, the B-45 Tornado.

As he unveiled his amazing story to me, I came to realize that there
are indeed miracles in life and that there are no real coincidences.

Throughout my life, I have been "successful" with a list of
accomplishments in education and career. But when I too had a crash
in my life, my dad's counsel helped me rebuild a life that would
bring me back to my Christian roots and balance my professional life
with my personal life. Dad taught me about enjoying the moment,
each and every one, every day.

99999999

INTRODUCTION

"When life is all sunshine and days are bright, our thoughts of the Lord may take wings of flight; But God is still ruler, His kingdom stands, and we all are subject to His commands."

— K. De Haan

I have been blessed throughout my life. I was born to good and loving parents and reared in a home filled with love, guidance, and empowerment.

It took me a long time to learn that I would be even more blessed if I were to mine the riches of my parents' past. My key to this treasure trove came in the form of a life crisis — we'll get to that in a minute — but first let me muse a bit about my parents' generation, the group whose life spans traversed most of the 20th century; the generation that NBC news anchor and author Tom Brokaw has famously labeled "The Greatest."

Tom was right, you know, not because this group was possessed of a superior genetic code, but because they happened to live during, and are shaped by, a unique period of our history, one that isn't likely to come about again. It was composed of dramatic downs and ups (yes, that's how it went for them) and exacerbated by a frenetically escalating pace of life itself, as amazing inventions, like television, began to change the world.

My mom and dad were among those stalwart sentinels of the 20th century who were children of the Depression, that aptly named period of economic and spiritual devastation that battered lives and scorched souls. My parents came of age during the Second World War, when men were eager to fight for freedom and perhaps their own tickets to move beyond their parents' simple, basic, and humble lifestyles. They were part of the generation that begat me along with millions of other babies.

The "Greatest Generation" developed a close bond as they banded together to protect America's freedoms— a bond they still share today.

Nearly all the able-bodied young men, actually boys for the most part, went off to war in the early 1940s. Many of the women left behind, young and old, put away their aprons, donned their work jackets and joined the labor force. It was absolutely necessary for the war effort. When the United States entered World War II, our military complex was ranked 18th in the world, behind Spain, the Netherlands, and Italy. Four years later, we were Number One. That's right, when Winston Churchill, Prime Minister of England, was pleading with President Franklin Delano Roosevelt to supply England with warships and planes, we were slow to step up to the plate. This was not only because of the preference of many in this country to "stay out of it," but also because we had next to nothing to offer; that changed radically in the early war years. Pearl Harbor saw to that: The events on December 7, 1941, signaled this nation that an isolationist policy just wouldn't fly in a world growing smaller and where other things did indeed fly — Japanese dive-bombers, for instance.

Fast forward to the war's conclusion: The young men — those who survived, that is — came home; the women dutifully handed over their jobs to the returning heroes; everyone got married, and before you knew it, they were Bringing up Baby. That would be me, and my brother, who came three years prior to my birth. And my fellow Boomers born between 1946 and 1962. Our parents happily showered us with toys they could only have dreamed of having during those bread-line years, and our Christmases were so very merry with Lionel trains and Betsy Wetsy dolls. Our plates ranneth over with the Four Food Groups and countless casseroles, and we got to go to Disneyland! Our moms read Dr. Spock; we read Dr. Seuss.

It was a fine childhood, filled with birthday parties, family vacations, and lots of travel, especially since I was the daughter of an Air Force pilot.

But for all the love and attention bestowed upon us kids, it wasn't until these many years later that I realized how little my mom and dad talked about their own lives. And I discovered, especially when I compared notes with my peers, just how typical this was of all our parents. And I got to wondering and speculating, why? Why didn't they share more of their trials and tribulations, their highs and lows? And how could so many of them emerge from their prolonged years of strife so strong in spirit?

My folks were born in the 1920s. During their lifetimes, their food was stored in iceboxes, then refrigerators; they witnessed the invention of so many things that I, and probably you, take for granted. I'm not talking just about television and computers. I'm thinking about things like plastic. Yes, plastic, that fills your medicine cabinets and wraps your food; today, when you drop a bottle of shampoo in the shower, it doesn't shatter. And plastic twist ties and garbage bags, grocery bags; plastic bumpers on cars and plastic casings on just about every modern appliance. Modern appliance? Now there's a term that wasn't in the vernacular of kids in the '30s, unless maybe you were referring to indoor plumbing. No wonder much of the living in those days was outside – lighting was sparse in small houses, and kitchens consisted of a sink, refrigerator, and gas or coal-burning stove. No microwaves, electric ovens, air conditioners, dishwashers, stereo systems, big screen TVs, or clothes dryers. No, the clothes were set out on the clothesline; even I have vivid memories in the '50s of helping my mom hang the shirts and pants, piece by piece. My job was to hand her two clothespins per item, and I was quite proficient at it, if I do say so myself.

In these "good old days," as we children are often prone to remember, a large portion of our time was spent playing games outdoors, like kick-the-can and tether ball. Those post-war houses were small; tract homes averaged about 900 square feet, and yet they could comfortably make room for Daddy, Mommy, their children, and a single television set. And the lucky families who got to move into those houses… they were grateful. Life after the challenges of WWII was good– "Lawrence Welk" for our parents and and "Leave It to Beaver" for us kids.

*I*NTRODUCTION

In the case of my military family, we didn't own a home in these years; we were always provided military housing as we moved from base to base. But the size and accoutrements, or lack thereof by today's standards, mirrored the times and we were quite satisfied with our abodes.

Again, I ask myself, why the lack of introspection among my parents' generation? Why did they hold their past inside? Or just not pay it much mind? I think, maybe, it had much to do with their pivotal point in our history. They watched their industrial-age parents and grandparents toil long, hard hours in factories, in coal mines or, like my dad's father, as a bricklayer. In those days, a penny saved was a penny earned. And then, as helpless little kids, they watched their hapless parents' pennies evaporate with the onset of the Great Depression.

The year 1933 found the Loudens among those families whose pocket books revealed nothing more than a few holes and worn leather. As a brick layer, my grandfather found it difficult to find work. Dad's family suffered financially as grandpa searched for a way to put food on the table and provide for his family. To survive, they used up all of their meager savings they had been accumulating for my dad's potential college, and eventually they had to tap into our nation's welfare system as well.

They needed a miracle or two during these trying times. It did indeed appear, as I recently discovered while interviewing my dad's cousin, Jack Wager, who is today a strong and dynamic 93-year-old.

During the depression, Jack had worked in his father's Ford dealership in Philadelphia. At the time, Ford was introducing their latest model with its new V8 engine. Ford ran a nationwide radio contest on the Lum and Abner show that aired every Friday evening. In 25 words or less, applicants were requested to submit a limerick that described why they would like to own the new Ford V8.

Jack wrote a limerick using each of the letters in the name FORD to begin his four sentences. Each line described a detail of the new Ford V8, which he was familiar with from the marketing literature they had received from Ford.

Of course, Jack couldn't submit the limerick because of his connection to the dealership. So, he did the next best thing—he sent it to his Uncle Frank and suggested he submit it. Grandpa did just that.

One exciting night in 1933 the Loudens were sitting around the family radio listening to the wonderful sounds that entertained my dad's generation. Then it happened. The miracle they so desperately needed filtered over the air waves and into the Louden family living room: The winner of the nationwide contest was Frank D. Louden of 214 Park Avenue in West View, Pennsylvania.

To this day, my dad remembers walking into the local Ford dealership with my grandpa Frank and picking out a brand new model Ford V8– in conservative black. What a wonderful gift. The car made it possible for grandpa to get to and from work and helped to relieve a financial hardship that swept the country during those difficult years.

It was a slow, hard climb out of the Depression and, truth be told, as awful as war is, that's what finally ignited their economy and the hope for a better tomorrow. And the survivors who came back from the war did indeed have that better tomorrow... an economy that began to hum and all the blessings that they hadn't dared to hope for began to come their way. Advances in medical care promised them longer lives. Consider, for example, that the average lifespan at the turn of the 19th to 20th century was a mere 40 years and that by the 1960s it was 72. Suddenly they had financial security – Social Security and Medicare – for those retirement years. They were able to buy homes, many for $1 as a veteran; often "modern" tract homes filled with all the latest conveniences wherein they raised those many children.

Oh, they must have felt lucky and grateful. And part of that gratitude must have told them, "now, don't you ever go feeling sorry for yourself." That would be self-indulgent, and their Depression upbringing steered them away from such "excesses."

And, besides, there just wasn't time to look back. The pace of life began speeding up, faster and faster, with automobiles and jet airplanes and telephones and bigger-and-bigger TVs and whirring blenders and coffee percolators and electric skillets. And it was compounded by more instantaneous communication of worldwide events: We entered a Cold War; the Berlin Wall went up; missiles were spotted in Cuba, and Khrushchev began banging his shoe. And there was a man on the moon and an assassination and the Reagan years and Perestroika and the Wall came down.

Never mind their reluctance to share their experiences, there simply wasn't time to look back. And we, their children, well... we were so busy keeping up with the pace of life and getting our advanced degrees and accumulating material goods, that we didn't have time to slow down and ask our folks much about their past.

That's how it was for me anyway. Until a small miracle happened. A life crisis that literally stopped me in my tracks. But it set me off on tracks into the past. I began a journey backward in time, and I uncovered buried family treasures that have since enriched my life.

I entered the world on July 2, 1953 in Nagoya, Japan, not so unusual given that my dad, James L. Louden, was a Major in the United States Air Force, stationed in Japan at the time.

My mom always said that I was too much of a firecracker to wait until the date my patriotic parents had most desired for my birth, the Fourth of July. Of course, every fun-loving American family enjoys this holiday, but let me tell you, if you're part of the military, it's a major event... Parades.

Parties that last all day. Red-white-and-blue bunting. Relay races. Fireworks. It's only natural that military families would revel in Independence Day festivities; they could take pride in having participated in this lasting legacy of freedom.

Later in life, I excused my early hatching by explaining to Mom and Dad that the "real" acceptance date of the Declaration of Independence was July 2, 1775 – they only signed it on the fourth. "Yes, dear," is about all I recall of my patient mother's reply. But I know some of that Independence Day spirit rubbed off on me in those early years, because I've always held a deep love for America along with an innate love of travel and adventure, history, and people. The constant change of addresses, even across continents that is so much of military life, was a lifestyle that I not only adapted to well, but also embraced.

As a youngster, I gladly soaked up each experience of living in or visiting exotic lands including Japan, Egypt, France, Greece, Italy, and Turkey. We had no television during our time in Europe and the Middle East, so my hours not spent in school focused on outdoor sports and an insatiable appetite for reading. Like my dad, some of my early readings inspired my future career choice, the world of business. I recall reading Ayn Rand's *Atlas Shrugged* in my early years, and having my first vision of a female executive – Dagny Taggart – who ran a major transcontinental railroad. In addition, my dad's sister, my Aunt Jean, set the stage for my eventual business career. She was a trailblazer in her time. Remaining single, she had a successful career in banking, moved from Pittsburgh to sunny Florida, was an avid golfer, and enjoyed her independent life. Role models – parents and our mentors – what a key role they play in forming our life direction and happiness.

Truly a type-A personality from the time I was a child, I thrived on constant motion of mind and body, and required minimal sleep. Blessed

with great genes, I was lucky to excel in many aspects of my life –
school, athletics, business. In 1975, I received a Bachelor of Science in
Applied Mathematics from North Carolina State University and two
years later, graduated with an MBA from the Darden School of
Business at the University of Virginia. An early pioneer in the expanding
women-in-business movement, I had little idea what roads I would
trail-blaze, but I was on my way.

By my late 20s, I had held significant positions, particularly for a young
woman. My medical career began in sales and marketing at Baxter Travenol
Laboratories. It was an exciting time to be with this rapidly expanding
Chicago-based medical technology company. Baxter had invented and
marketed the revolutionary plastic IV bag. I was able to participate in
what became the mass movement to plastic medical disposable products.
I subsequently was a health care consultant with Booz, Allen & Hamilton
and then served as Director of Corporate Strategic Planning for American
Hospital Supply Corporation, at that time the nation's largest distributor
of medical supplies.

By age 29, I found corporate America with its rigid hierarchy and
bureaucratic policies and procedures to be too constraining, and in 1983,
I excitedly launched my own health care marketing and strategy consulting
firm in downtown Chicago. With the public relations skills I inherited
from my dad, my consulting practice flourished.

What I didn't start out with, money, I more than made up for with
my driven personality along with public speaking and sales capabilities.
The Louden Network took off quickly and soon became nationally
recognized as I published articles and industry studies, spoke at hundreds
of industry conferences, and was quoted in The Wall Street Journal and
leading health care publications. I was just past age 30 when I was selected
as one of Crain's Business Chicago magazine's 40 under 40 award

winners – what a high that was. Needless to say, I worked excessive hours and, like so many of my fellow friends, took on the yuppie obsession with running, running, and running! Whether rain, sleet, snow, ice, or 100 degree days – that daily run was a necessity and a badge of success.

While I didn't know it at the time, looking back, it's no wonder I was headed for a physical crash. Most of the time, we don't see these things coming until it's too late. The long hours of work, excessive travel, corporate entertaining, lack of sleep, and my running mania had at last stressed my otherwise energetic body. God gave me the only message I would have listened to in order to slow down. I had no choice.

MY CRASH

*"Strength does not come from physical capacity.
It comes from an indomitable will."*

— Mohandas K. Gandhi

It was early December 1997, and I was finally feeling better after two weeks of being down-and-out with a major case of the Asian flu that had descended upon Chicago. I had never been this sick before, and the flu hit me hard. I was flat on my back for two solid weeks, an unheard of length of time for this type-A personality to be out of action.

Unable to keep food or drink down, I had lost 15 pounds. I weighed in at 99 pounds, and I was as weak as I had ever been in my life.

Now on the mend, I felt great to be able to eat a bagel and an apple and drink some tea. Oh, yeah, I was "back." It was time to pick up where I had left off earlier that month, the busy month of December, a favorite time of year for me. One of the joys of living high above the Chicago lakefront, and a major reason I chose this lifestyle, was to be able to entertain, inviting friends over for holiday parties and a birds-eye view of the snow-covered trees around Michigan Avenue and its historic Water Tower. Maybe there would still be time to think about a little soiree just after the New Year...

Today, I was ready to resume my usual routine and eager to breathe fresh air after having been cooped up day after day. I was actually looking forward to braving the chill of a winter morning in the Windy City.

I hopped into the elevator of my high-rise condo building, descended to the lobby, made my re-acquaintance with our building's doorman and was soon running my regular route along the lakefront.

I had run four miles and in the biting cold was feeling no pain; indeed, I had even reconnected with my old "runner's high" in which I felt the oxygen flowing throughout my body and entered almost a meditative zone. I was on my final stretch, wind at my back, sailing past the Drake Hotel, when something snapped.

I was suddenly hit with a seething pain in my hips and lower back. It literally stopped me in my tracks. As I would discover in the days, weeks, months, and years to follow, this pain would mark a 45-degree turn in my life, which was, coincidentally, nearing its 45th year.

Bent over, I struggled to return to my condo, while shooting, almost electrical, jolts ricocheted through my limbs. It was so cold that the tears I shed froze on my face. Once inside my door, I collapsed on the floor in excruciating pain.

And then I sobbed. I cried more than I ever had in my life. Tears of fear, and screams of agony, gave voice to the throbbing pain that ripped through my back and seared from my hips. I cried so hard I couldn't catch my breath, and the sobs themselves would inevitably cause my body to shake and that would cause the pain to reverberate more. I was terrified. Given my experience in the medical industry, I knew that this was something very serious. It was beyond my control. And I had always been in control.

In-control and in-command Teri. Independent Teri, constantly in motion physically and mentally, with an unending supply of energy. My life had been so blessed up to this point.

With my medical experience and strong network, I had no trouble connecting with top physicians in Chicago. My first call was made to a friend, Anne Kerstetter Feldstein, who had been a senior executive at the Rehabilitation Institute of Chicago. It was a Sunday, and she made the right calls to allow me to see a top physical medicine physician first thing Monday morning. In health care, as in life, it pays to have connections. But, even the best connections can't help in some medical situations — in the end, the individual must take charge of their own health care and healing.

Needless to say, New Year's Eve 1997 was not ushered in with great cheer. I dreaded thinking of the tough times that lay ahead for me to heal and recuperate.

Standing was bearable, but sitting was next to impossible. Sleep deprivation became an all too common reality. In the months ahead, I went through a string of doctors as I searched for an answer and a cure. They both proved to be quite illusive.

As I shuttled from doctor to doctor, I was poked, prodded, and analyzed. I saw an orthopedic surgeon, a neurologist, a neurosurgeon, a physical medicine physician, and an anesthesiologist. Referrals to physical therapists found me stretched in many directions on floor mats only to arrive home in more pain than before. I became reconciled to the fact that chronic pain would be part of my future.

Pain medications, some of them quite strong, were an obvious prescription, and many were suggested to me. But with a business to run, staff to manage and support, and clients to serve, painkillers weren't an option for me; they might deaden the pain, but they'd leave me drowsy and incapable of working. It's a good thing I had my trusty dog Sam to help take my mind off the pain.

As a strategy consultant in the medical industry, one of the emerging trends I had been following was the melding of Eastern and Western medicines. My research left me with a better understanding of the mind-body connection and alternative treatments that could make a difference when our traditional Western medical approaches fail to deliver. And, in my case, this was painfully true. This blending of medical practice and ancient philosophies would come to play an integral part in my healing.

Saying goodbye to The Windy City… Thanks for the memories.

At the time, I didn't realize I had inherited my dad's great mindset of "moving on" rather than dwelling on problems. Today, I thank the Good Lord for this mindset, as it proved instrumental for my eventual healing. I made a key decision to relocate to a warmer, more comfortable climate and one less stressful than living on Michigan Avenue in downtown Chicago. If I were to be in chronic pain for the rest of my life, I reasoned I would endure it better in a warmer and quieter location, and one that would put me in closer touch with the healing powers of nature.

A farewell Chicago River ride with Dad.

My longtime Chicago friends could not believe I was serious about leaving. I had lived in the city over 15 years, the longest time I had lived in one location. But even in that city, with my adventuresome spirit, I had moved seven times.

4

San Diego… Ready for new adventures.

I loved Chicago, and always will. As they say, there is a time and a place for everything – it was time for me to move on.

Throughout my professional career, I had traveled extensively to speak at medical conferences and executive retreats in all parts of the country, including several in San Diego and the resort community of Coronado, just across San Diego Bay. Known for the Hotel Del Coronado, a famous historic oceanfront resort hotel, Coronado, a casual small-town village, is home to one of the most beautiful stretches of beach in all of the U.S. I remembered my special times there after my presentations. There was nothing better than walking the beach and enjoying the beautiful sunsets. I enjoyed the relaxed pace of this community, filled with flowers, sunshine, and classic Southern California sunsets. I decided to make it home and eventually found a place on the ocean.

Coronado, with its fitting nickname "The Enchanted Island," is the type of place where people dream of someday retiring. But, I asked myself, why wait? In your later years it could be too late to really enjoy your chosen retirement location and more difficult to develop a support group of friends. By making the move to Coronado in my relatively younger years, I was also making a decision to live in the moment. That philosophy made

it much easier to enhance my mental attitude, prepare for the future and, of course, cope with my immediate concern, chronic pain.

Soon after settling in Coronado, the power of following God's will and my

Teri, Ms. Willis and Sam enjoy their new beach office in front of the Hotel Del Coronado. —*photo by Vernon Jacobs*

heart became clear to me. I've come to believe that there really aren't any coincidences in life; instead there is a higher power handing us serendipitous moments. SQuire Rushnell, who served as an executive with ABC and led Good Morning America to a number-one rating, calls life's coincidences "God Winks" in his book *When God Winks*. I, by no accident, found this book when I needed it most.

I had grown up in a Christian home; we went to church on Sunday, and my parents often referred to Biblical stories to teach my brother and me about the importance of living a good Christian life. But as I got caught up in the business world, there didn't seem to be enough time to reflect on the Bible or Christian philosophy. However, as I was forced to stop and reflect during my injury, my childhood teachings would come back to me in profound ways. I soon found God winking and blinking and batting his eyes at me. It had been happening all my life; I just had not taken the time to open my eyes to see it.

For example, while setting up house in Coronado, I ordered a modular office-furniture system and soon became friends with the sales representative. As I related my story, she shared that her husband had suffered from similar hip and back pain and had found relief through chiropractic medicine.

Soon, he and I were in touch, and I followed his advice and direction; this visit to a chiropractor marked my first venture away from traditional medicine. At long last, I secured an accurate diagnosis of my problem— a sprained sacrum that meant my weak and torn ligaments weren't holding my hips together. In turn, this created hip imbalance and severe pressure on nerves up and down my spine and throughout my hips and legs. The chiropractor strongly advised me to begin the healing process by not moving for three months, at the very least. It was exactly the opposite advice I had been following for the many months since my injury.

Meditating on Coronado Beach. —photo by Chad Thompson

For a person always on the move, being told not to move was a challenge in itself. Not "doing" something had always seemed to me to be wasteful and frivolous. Now, as I began to experience the power of "stillness" in this alternative path, I began to investigate, with my characteristic zeal, other wellness and health options; therapeutic Pilates, yoga, and meditation unveiled a new world of understanding for me.

Gradually, I began to feel better and I mistook this as a signal to push and overdid my exercise. Not surprisingly, this resulted in a re-injury. In its

Teri and Dad relax at the beach.

way, my body was teaching me to slow down, both mentally and physically — otherwise I would have to face serious consequences. If I were to move without pain in the future, I would have to learn how to slow down, relax, and take my mind and body to a less-active place.

I was forced to turn to others to help me through this journey. When you're incapacitated as I was, you need to reach out to others for hope.

There is a saying that when the student is ready, the teacher appears, and this rang true for me. My first teacher was Dan, my chiropractor. My second teacher was Bruno, a wonderful Pilates instructor in San Diego. Bruno gave me hope because he had experienced my same injury. But, this hope was dim, as he said it would take up to five years for me to recuperate. He prescribed a strong dosage of inactivity.

I thank the Good Lord for sending me a messenger that I would listen to. It actually took me six years, not five. Ironically, the person closest to me turned out to be my third teacher. That teacher was my dad.

It occurred to me that he might have some answers because of his recovery from a plane crash that had happened before I was born. During our long coast-to-coast telephone talks, Dad told me that since his crash in a B-45 jet bomber 50 years earlier, he had lived and breathed chronic pain, agonizing at times. I invited him to visit me for the month of December 1999.

I grew up not knowing much about his pain or the details surrounding the crash, as my parents were reluctant to discuss the event, likely not wanting to remember the stressful and life-threatening ordeal.

Coronado, surf and sand.

Interview kick-off dinner.

My dad arrived to enjoy the holidays with me at my new home at the Coronado Shores resort condominiums. Known locally as "The Shores," this complex of ten, high-rise buildings is the tallest landmark in Coronado. My penthouse not only allowed Dad and me to take in panoramic views of the Pacific, it also afforded us a front-row seat to view the holiday display next door at the Hotel Del Coronado; the hotel's red Victorian

9

Popping the cork for the new Millennium.

architecture, including turrets and cupolas, was outlined nightly throughout the season with sparkling white lights. Every night at 5:00 p.m. sharp, we enjoyed our personal light show, a very special gift for our holiday celebrations.

But what Dad really enjoyed was watching Navy pilots practice touch-and-go landings at Naval Air Station, North Island. Jet fighters would come in off the water directly in front of my condo, then head in for final approach following the coastline up to the landing lights at the air station.

Though neither of us realized it at the time, this visit and subsequent visits provided rare opportunities for a dad and daughter to connect on a deeper level. I thought I was wise and worldly, but my thinking changed dramatically as I began the most extended visit I had ever had with him.

My dad served as my coach, teaching me how to live through every day with pain and injury. He taught, not by lecturing, but by demonstrating his techniques of relaxing, meditating, and spiritual practices. Relishing every moment of every day, he contentedly sat in my comfortable living room chair, watching beachgoers and meditating before a setting sun. He would invite me to slow down, if only for half an hour to appreciate the beautiful sunsets.

"Don't worry about anything, Teri," Dad said to me, and I must say I was really in a worrying state as I wondered if I would ever be able to exercise or travel again.

Dad said, "Just pray to the good Lord, put your faith in Jesus Christ, and he'll be there for you. I'm a child of God; you're a child of God — trust in God and then relax."

Dad did relax. He relished those sunsets and played his harmonica.

Harmonica at sunset.

I admitted to him and to myself how difficult this was for me. By the time he left, I began to realize the benefit and enjoyment of gifting myself the healing experience of such quiet contemplation.

My dad and I bonded in an exceptional way during this extended time together, and I discovered we shared a deep connection. We both, for the first time, realized that we were two peas in a pod. I was indeed more like my dad than I had ever imagined. After all, in my generation, it was more likely for a daughter to follow in her mother's footsteps. But anyone who knows me will say that I am my father's daughter.

I'd have to say my upbringing was pretty typical for a mid-20th century family. My mother, a "stay-at-home" mom, when that phrase was not yet in vogue, was a consistent presence for my brother and me. Dad was "the provider," busy with work, which took him away a lot. And when you're in the military, "away" means away. On two tours of military duty, Dad was gone for a year at a time. And even when he was stationed locally, Dad was a busy guy. Oh, we had lots of time together as a family — fun and memorable times that included vacations, sporting events, picnics, bowling leagues, military parades, holiday celebrations at the base club, church outings, and concerts. But there wasn't much one-on-one time for a dad and a daughter.

We didn't have discussions about my life, goals, aspirations, or challenges. These discussions, if at all, were with my mother. I suppose this was typical with many father-daughter relationships of my parents' generation. Dad happily praised me for the skills I acquired around the house – cleaning, baking, ironing his countless military shirts, and helping my mother entertain. I was praised for consistent good grades and staying in excellent physical health.

Dad was supportive and rather amazed when I graduated from college with a degree in applied mathematics. He was further dumbfounded when I announced I intended to get an MBA. I still remember his question: "What's an MBA?" Need I say more?

Later in life, he was proud of my accomplishments. As I entered the business world and subsequently started my own company, his interest in my professional life grew, and he became the proud father spurring me on.

As I interviewed my dad about his mindset in overcoming and managing pain and disability, details emerged about his life. For the first time, he told me the details of the harrowing story about his crash in a B-45 jet bomber and miracle survival, his military career, and his life philosophies and rituals, including his daily spiritual practice of prayer and giving thanks to the Lord. He told me how it is possible to be happy every moment of every day.

He brought with him detailed family scrapbooks and photo albums that my mother had meticulously pieced together over the years, documenting our travels, our

Teri surprises Dad on his 80th.

12

military life, and dad's crash. Somehow, I believe that she too wanted *On God's Wings* to be written to preserve the facts, the photos, and the many blessings we have enjoyed as a family.

Dad helped me consider and make some significant changes to slow down my pace, take more time to rest and relax, add prayer and meditation to my daily life, commit to a daily yoga practice, walk on the beach more, smell the roses, and spend time nurturing good friendships.

Spa time with Dad helps Teri on her road to recovery.

My father's visits gave me a jumpstart on a new approach to life. While his lessons did not produce an overt, immediate change (type As are tough to slow down), Dad's simple teachings served as a guiding light for a grateful daughter toward a breaking dawn of peace and contentment.

Along my road to recovery, my dad and I experienced the fun and relaxation of father-daughter time at health spas. He put his trust in me at our first spa week together — this was a new experience even for my otherwise adventurous dad. But after a week of massage, facials, relaxing swims and time in the hot tub, he changed his mind about health spas being only for the ladies. Thereafter, spa times became an ongoing ritual for us, and we continue to have fun planning our next spa experience.

While traditionally mothers and daughters have enjoyed special spa times together, I highly recommend including dad on your next spa trip.

Today, as my alternative physical pursuits of yoga and Pilates allow me to keep chronic pain from my body while maintaining physical exercise, my father's lessons have helped me to lead a more balanced life.

I am hopeful that my father's story will encourage others to learn more about their parents' lives and, in turn, obtain valuable lessons for themselves and future generations.

"Dancer Pose" in front of The Hotel Del Coronado. —photo by Chad Thompson

Enjoying yoga and life— free of pain at last. —photo by Chad Thompson

ON GOD'S WINGS

THE EARLY YEARS

*"Once you have tasted flight, you will forever walk the earth with
your eyes turned skyward, for there you have been, and there you
will always long to return."*

— Leonardo da Vinci

"You know, Teri, my birthday is now a national holiday," says Dad with a chuckle.

Dad was born in 1921 on January 15, the same day as Martin Luther King. And just as Dr. King's life was fueled with a passion for human rights, my dad is a living testament to a life focused on loving every human being no matter what nationality, race, creed, or color. I thank him for passing this life lesson on to me.

Same smile, little four-year-old Jim.

He was eight-years-old when he developed a love for baseball and flying. He was younger still when he picked up a harmonica and taught himself to play; it has been his musical instrument of choice for the past eight decades.

Dad grew up in a small community, West View, about seven miles north of Pittsburgh, Pennsylvania. He had dreams beyond the town's horizons, and he found himself on the pathway toward those dreams through reading books.

One of the earliest books he read was the Bible, and, as a child, he was assigned a Bible verse by the Rev. Luther P. Spoehr at St. Luke's Evangelical Lutheran Church that became his lifelong benchmark:

> *"Ask, and it shall be given you; Seek, and ye shall find;*
> *Knock, and it shall be opened unto you."*
>
> — Matthew 7:7

At five-years-old, Dad's parents gave him some pennies, and he used them to buy himself a 10-hole Marine-band harmonica. It was made by Hohner of Germany and was the best harmonica money could buy. Young Jim often listened to the radio and loved the music of the "Harmonicats." He decided he would learn to play just like them. Over the many years to follow, the harmonica became his trademark and his great connection with people all over the world. His musical talent would play a major role in his life to attract and uplift people. Even today, he is eager to bring joy to others and never hesitates to take advantage of any opportunity to perform. Over the years, he has built up quite a repertoire of tunes that include songs of the World War II era, military songs, religious hymns, and, of course, God Bless America and Take Me Out to the Ballgame.

My dad is a terrific example of the impact that books can have on a youngster's life.

The Pride of the Yankees, a book by Lou Gehrig, churned his fervor to be a major league baseball player. Early on in his life, he developed a mindset that inspired a "you-can-do-whatever-you-aspire-to" attitude.

In 1929, eight-year-old Jim sat down with a lofty read, *Air Power of World War I*, written by World War I Flying Ace Billy Mitchell. His mind drifted skyward: One day he would become a pilot. He would seek that.

When he was a little boy of ten, two airplane rides stimulated his passion to be a pilot. The first was in an old tri-model aluminum airplane with three engines made by the Ford Motor Company. Jim took a $1 ride around Bettis Airport in Pittsburgh. A buck back in the early '30s was a lot of money, especially to a ten-year-old kid. He loved flying, and knew he really wanted to be a pilot. A few months later, he went out to a small airport with a grass strip just north of Pittsburgh. Another dollar bill bought him a ride on a Stearman bi-plane. That was it. He had twice experienced the thrill of flying that he had read about, dreamed about.

Jim plays ball. Keating Volunteer Fire Department sponsored baseball team, 1941.

Even before his dreams of being a pilot, Jim had visions of making it in the big league world of baseball. In his early years, he took two streetcars to the old Pittsburgh Pirates Stadium, Forbes Field. There he sold peanuts to pay for his streetcar rides and watched the games for free while yelling, "PEA-NUTS!"

Jim had played high school baseball and upon seeing his skill and passion, his coach encouraged him to try out for the Pirates. "You've got the potential, kid, to make it in the majors as a home-run hitter."

Jim, who had now grown to his full stature of 6 foot, 2 inches, traveled by streetcar to the tryouts for five days straight. Only six contracts were available to the 400 candidates. Jim made it through to the very last day, before he got axed, with the scouts telling him his arm wasn't yet strong enough for the big leagues. But they suggested he try again in two years.

"It was tough," Jim admits today. "I knew I had real trouble with that curveball and wasn't sure things would improve in two years. But I gave it my best, and went pretty far. And not being on a major league team didn't mean baseball would be out of my life. I still had another passion to push to the front burner — my love of flying. It was time to move on."

Dad still loves baseball today; he played a lot of amateur baseball in the Air Force as he traveled the world. He loved coming to Chicago and going to Wrigley Field and Comiskey Park with me and my friends. He now enjoys the new Padres Stadium, PETCO Park, in San Diego when he visits me.

During the summer of 1939, Jim recalls entering a recruiting office in downtown Pittsburgh.

"Do you have any openings at any air base in the country where I can start my flying training and become a pilot?" he asked them.

"Yeah, we've got an opening for an aerial photographer at Lowry Field in Denver that would be ideal for you to get your aviation experience."

"I'll take it."

One hitch: The recruiter informed Jim that he couldn't accept an 18-year-old without parental permission.

"Okay, give me the paperwork, and I'll take it home."

But Dad's father had served in the infantry in France during World War I and had a fresh memory of what combat was about. He refused to sign.

"Son, war is h-e-l-l," he told him. "When you're 21, you can do what you want, but I'm not signing."

Jim was disappointed and angry.

"Man, that was rough. But as I look back, I know he probably saved my life," Jim says today. "If I had signed on then, chances are I would have ended up on the front lines and never returned home."

But three years later when he turned 21, Jim realized he had the

Jim's dad, Frank, age 24 in WWI, 1918.

right stuff for flying. It was June 6, 1942, just six months after Pearl Harbor, when Jim enlisted in the U.S. Army.

He reported to Fort Lee, Virginia, for eight weeks of Army basic training with no immediate plans to take to the skies. One day while hauling rocks, Jim heard buzzing in the sky, looked up and spied an Army Air Corps DC-3 flying overhead. The "Old Gooney Bird," manufactured in 1932 by Douglas Aircraft and still in existence today, stirred his senses.

"My God, I wish I was up there flying that plane instead of down here hauling rocks," Jim shouted to God and anyone in hearing distance. "I'm getting my ass down to the recruiting house today to see if I can sign up for aviation cadet training and get the hell out of here."

And, he did.

"Teri, when I enlisted in the Army, I had no promise that I'd be able to fly, but I took a chance," Dad told me. "I didn't have a college education. But they didn't care because the Army Air Corps was desperate. Anyone who could pass both the mental and physical tests was accepted."

Cadets in training. Garner Field, Uvalde, TX, Feb. 1943. Back row: Cecil Boyer, Jr.; George M. Houston; McGaffigan; Front row: Chas R. Lynch (Pinky); Jim Louden.

They were tough and arduous tests, but Dad scored well on both, and was off to the Lone Star State for eight weeks of pre-flight training at Kelly Field in San Antonio, Texas. As an aviation cadet, he studied aerodynamics, weather, theory of flight, history of aviation, and design of airplane engines.

Did he find it was as much fun as he had thought?

"It got better each day as a new adventure and chapter unfolded," Jim remembers. He passed all the mental and physical exams with flying colors.

"Following just ten hours of training, they sent me up on a solo," he remembers vividly. "And it was sweet. I was in the heavens."

He was also in a PT-19, a brand new low-wing, monoplane made by Fairchild Aviation of Hagerstown, Maryland.

Kelly Field was also the site of Cadet Louden's first solo flight in a BT-9, an exciting airplane made by North American Aviation with a 450-horse-power engine and no retractable landing gear. Coincidentally, North American Aviation manufactured the B-45 airplane that awaited his destiny in 1949. Jim's civilian instructor cautioned him that if he ever had to make an emergency landing, to make sure he rolled back the glass canopy so he wouldn't be caught under it and cut to death. At 1,000 feet above ground, Jim was in trouble – the BT-9's engine suddenly quit. Quickly, he commenced an instrument check. Everything, including fuel, registered okay, but meanwhile, the airplane was falling like a rock. As the ground moved closer, Jim remembered his instructor's advice and rolled back the canopy. He made a beeline for a nearby field and headed in for his first emergency crash landing.

The airplane hit, bounced hard, and bounced again fifteen or twenty feet straight up. Then it came down on its nose and flipped over. The next thing Jim knew, the airplane was on top of him, and he was in the mud. He had to dig out like a rabbit from underneath the cockpit, and run full speed, in case the airplane exploded. Rushed in an ambulance to the hospital for a thorough checkup, Jim surprisingly did not have a scratch on him. The doctors asked how he felt about flying again as they were going to send him back up the next morning before he developed a fear of flying. He said he wanted to go again. True to their words, the next morning, he was up soloing again and loving every moment.

The plane's aeronautical records showed a prior history of maintenance problems over many months. The crash was written off as 100 percent mechanical failure with no pilot error. It wouldn't be the last time mechanical failure would come face to face with pilot Jim Louden.

Jim with his aviation cadet buddies.
Lewis Latas, left, & Richard McLachlan, right.
Goodfellow Field, April 6, 1943.

Next up was advanced training in the summer of 1943 at Ellington Field in Houston in a twin-engine, low-wing monoplane, the AT-9, made by Curtis, one of the fastest training planes in the Air Corps at the time. The Army Air Corps was preparing Jim for the plane he would fly once he got his wings.

B-26 Martin Marauder, world's fastest bomber - 400 mph, 1940.

When asked what three types of aircraft he'd like to fly, Jim chose a P-38 Lightning, an A-20 Havoc, and the B-25 Billy Mitchell made by North American. But because the Army Air Corps was desperate for pilots who could handle the B-26 Martin Marauder, this was the aircraft assigned to him.

Due to numerous crashes, the B-26 had earned a bad reputation and such colorful monikers as "The Flying Prostitute," "Widow Maker," and "The Baltimore Whore." And because it had no visible means of support for a wingspan of 69 feet, it was also known as "The Flying Coffin."

The B-26 was tough to fly and made men out of boys in a hurry. In pilot circles, it was said that if you can fly a Marauder, you can fly anything. No matter where in the world you were flying this plane, it had to come in on final approach at 150 miles an hour with no reverse thrust.

Proud Jim with his new cadet wings, May 1943.

"Runways of the era were 4,000 to 5,000-feet long, not the 9,000 to 12,000-footers in use today, so landings were intense," Jim remembers.

James Louden got his wings and was commissioned a 2nd Lieutenant on July 29, 1943 at Ellington Field, Houston. And with his wings came one of the nicknames that would stay with him the rest of his life, "Big Jim." He was a tall, strapping guy. But his moniker went beyond his physicality; his easy manner and self-assurance bred confidence among his peers.

He became "larger than life" in their eyes and many crewmen wanted to fly with "Big Jim."

"Big Jim's" first assignment was in Del Rio, Texas, where he learned to fly the B-26 Marauder. But first, during his initial two-week leave back in Pittsburgh, he'd have the opportunity to show off his shiny new wings pinned proudly on his chest.

As war was being fought both in the South Pacific and Europe, a man in uniform was highly regarded. Pilots were heroes and the uniform attracted the girls. But this young man's eyes were on one girl only – Margaret (Peggy) Neuner. He fondly remembered the effect she had had on him when he first laid eyes on her four years earlier while he was working as a Mellon Bank messenger boy. At one of his

Peggy Neuner caught the eyes of Big Jim in 1943.

stops, he had noticed her, a telephone operator and receptionist, at Singer Iron and Steel, a scrap-iron company in downtown Pittsburgh.

His first thought was, "My God, she's beautiful. Someday I'd like to marry that girl," Jim remembers clear as day.

Peggy was as petite as Jim was tall. A full foot separated them in height. She stood 5 feet 2 inches and weighed just over 100 pounds. She was a pretty brunette with flawless milky skin and deep-set brown eyes. He was tall and strong, a 6-feet-2-inch handsome "gung ho" guy with a tireless smile.

Peggy never left his consciousness, and now, home on his first leave, Jim called to ask Peggy out. Tommy Dorsey was in town with his big band that included Gene Krupa on the drums, performing at the William Penn Hotel. Peggy's father answered the telephone and Jim boldly informed him that he was Lt. Jim Louden, just got his wings, was home on vacation for a few days, and wondered if Peggy had a boyfriend. He informed my dad that, yes, she had a boyfriend, and it was he – her dad.

Mom Sarah and dad Frank show pride in their newly uniformed son, July 1942.

Peggy's dad liked Jim from the start and teased him unmercifully. This did not stray the Lieutenant, who left his number for the young lady. Peggy did call. She declared she was engaged to an Army officer stationed in France and professed to vaguely remember Jim. Not dissuaded at all, Jim convinced Peggy to go to a movie with him, slyly disclosing that he had his wings and was a new second lieutenant. Eventually, he wooed her to his way of thinking with help from her parents, whom he won over with

Jim and Peggy, just married, Dec. 15, 1945.

his fun-loving personality, positive attitude, and, of course, his harmonica.

That was the beginning of a romance that was united in marriage on December 15, 1945, in Pittsburgh. Jim and Peggy had forty-eight years together traveling the world, celebrating life, and raising two children – a son, James, Jr., and me, Teri.

Returning to Del Rio after his leave home, Jim commenced two months of intensive training on flying the B-26 Marauder. After twelve hours with an instructor, Jim was allowed to fly solo. He passed triumphantly on everything including instrument checks.

"You're a natural-born pilot," said his instructor, "you'll have no problem."

This was to be prophetic, as Jim would eventually accumulate over 6,000 hours in almost twenty types of aircraft; 600 of which would be in combat.

Learning to master the B-26 on one engine, with simulated single-engine takeoffs, was challenging and required incredible skill. This beautifully designed plane was equipped with two R2800 Pratt & Whitney engines with four-bladed props. The B-26 would earn the best combat-loss record, less than one-half of one percent, of any bomber in World War II. The plane carried 4,000 pounds of bombs that could be dropped from 10,000 feet, a far cry from the B-24s and B-17s that had to stay at 25,000 to 30,000 feet. The bombing record of the Marauders in World War II was outstanding.

Next, Jim was transferred to his first bomb group, the 397th, at MacDill Air Force Base in Tampa, Florida. On the bombing ranges there, he practiced skip and low-altitude bombing. Just before being sent overseas, the group went to Hunter Field in Savannah, Georgia, for two weeks of pre-combat training, strafing the shoreline there. Next, at Camp Atterbury, Indiana, he dropped bombs on practice ranges and practiced low-level skip bombing for another two weeks.

In March 1944, it was time to go. Since he had joined the bomb group late, air crews had already been formed to fly the airplanes over to England, and Jim had to take the slow boat, an Italian vessel that had been converted into a troop transport. Navy destroyers escorted the ship across the Atlantic to scout out German U-boats that were looking to seek and destroy the transport ship. The destroyers were positioned just off the bow on either side of Jim's ship, and went after the submarines they spotted by dropping depth charges. The U-boat threat necessitated the ship to change course every ten seconds all the way across the ocean, stretching the voyage to thirteen days before reaching Scotland.

Disembarking at 4 a.m., a weary Lt. Louden boarded a train that took him to Braintree, England where he reported the next day to the 397th Bomb Group. He was immediately assigned a crew and began pre-combat training.

On April 20, 1944, the first combat mission of the 397th Medium Bomb Group Flying Marauders occurred.

"I felt fortunate to be included on that first combat mission," Jim said. "I was filled with incredible pride."

Jim was still young but had come a long way to defining his life by pursuing his passions. He had made beautiful music on his harmonica, pursued a baseball career, moved on to flying, and won the girl of his dreams. The doors he knocked upon were opened unto him.

"I followed my passions," Jim says. "It's how I got through to the Army recruiters, to Peggy's parents, and to my beloved Peggy. When you are passionate, you are sincere. Sincerity counts; people see it, feel it, hear it. Pursue your passions, Teri. Pray for direction and guidance throughout your life and use your God-given talents to their maximum. Seek and ye shall find."

WORLD WAR II, D-DAY

"Do not anticipate trouble, or worry about what may never happen. Keep in the sunlight."

— Benjamin Franklin

Jim Louden's first D-Day mission started early in the morning. They were making a beeline to France, occupied by the Germans. The group would have just a couple of hours to reach the target, Utah Beach, drop the bombs and get back safely.

The 397th, known as the "Bridge Busters," specialized in knocking out bridges behind the German lines to support the Allied troops. They participated in various missions during pivotal campaigns with the bombing occurring behind the German lines, bombing bridges and marshalling yards to prevent them from bringing ammunition and supplies up to the troops.

Pilot Big Jim, left, with his crew of the B-26 Martin Marauder. Dec. 6, 1944.

Their second target was a marshalling railroad yard not far from the city of St. Lo. The yard was a vital target, housing the German's transportation depot supply for troops, armaments, and equipment.

As they approached the depot at an elevation of 10,000 feet, puffs of black smoke from artillery shells, "flak," exploded all around them. Jim could clearly see the flak bursting not far from his cockpit. It scared the hell out of him.

But one of the things Jim liked best about the B-26 Marauder was its maneuverability; it was one of the hottest of the medium-sized bombers made in the USA. This fast plane had quite a reputation for making dynamic and shifty moves, but the fast plane required equally fast flyers like Big Jim. He could lay the plane on its side and dive down from high altitudes, climb, swerve, and continually outwit and confound the enemy.

But the last thirty seconds over target was a different story. To ensure that the bombs hit their target, the heading and the altitude had to be held constant. Regardless of how close to his plane the shells were detonating, Jim had to keep flying straight. During those long 30 seconds, Jim's plane and all planes of the 397th would be sitting ducks.

"Bombs Away! Hearing those words in my headset were the sweetest sounds I'd ever hear," Jim recalled, noting this high sign from the bombardier was his signal to "get the hell out of there."

He immediately made a 90-degree diving turn. Looking back to the spot where his plane had been only moments before, Jim saw heavy-duty flak exploding.

But he was on his way home and took a moment to run his fingers across his two good luck charms: his uncle's World War I U.S. Marine dog tag and a little cross from a Catholic friend that was supposed to keep him safe at all times.

599TH BOMBARDMENT SQUADRON

Jim Louden's 397th Bomb Group in WWII was in the 599th Bomb Squadron. As with all air squadrons, their aircraft marking was more than an insignia. It was and remains a symbol of their pride. The beaver inspired strength and courage in these men, many whose lives were given for the freedom of our great country. To this day, when the 397th gets together, they hang their banner high, displaying the beaver with remembrance and reverence. The insignia was originally commissioned in June of 1944 with the following details: "Over and through a light blue green disc, border black, a caricatured beaver with look of ferocity on face, having human 'strong man's' body tan, wearing light red boxing trunks, white belt and blue sleeveless jersey marked on chest with winged beaver head and white shoes and gloves, carrying a large, black aerial bomb, highlighted of the field, on the right shoulder and a black, aerial machine gun in the left hand, highlighted of the field, all casting black drop shadow to Dexter." The insignia faced toward the front of the aircraft.

The charms worked, Jim thought. He was back safely with two D-Day missions under his belt.

The B-26 Martin Marauder had a more limited fuel capacity than the other bombers, so the pilots weren't able to penetrate deep into German territory. Because their missions were shorter, Marauder pilots started with a 50-mission limit. The limit for B-17 and B-24 planes, capable of longer duration flights, was 25 missions. Before it was all over, Jim exceeded the limit and completed 64 combat missions in the B-26.

The highlights of Jim's combat flying over England and France were his D-Day missions on June 6, 1944. He would never forget that day. The group knew that D-Day was fast approaching because they were busy participating in preparatory operations to the Normandy invasion, attacking weapon sites, bridges, coastal defenses, marshalling yards, and airfields.

Rumors started flying around the base that tomorrow was the day. Brigadier General Sam Anderson arrived at 3 a.m. to brief them.

"This is it, boys. This is what you've been training for over the last year. You're going into real combat this morning; it's D-Day," Anderson said solemnly. "General Eisenhower has ordered you to go, and you'll go as low as you have to and drop bombs on Utah Beach.

"There will be no dropping of bombs through the clouds today. You have to see your target because those boys wading ashore are depending on you."

It was raining hard that morning; terrible, stormy weather, but there was no turning back. Each airplane had a red Aldus lamp in the tail and took off in the driving rain, fifteen seconds behind the plane before them. A total of 36 planes took off in two box formations. Jim was in the second formation, flying number two. He was selected to be on the right wing of his squadron commander, Major Crabtree, and Crabtree's number-two man. Louden respected the Major as a tremendous combat leader.

His respect and caring for the Major lasted a lifetime. If anything happened to the Major's plane that morning, Jim would have taken over the formation.

Following those red lamps in the tails of the airplanes was their saving grace. That's how they were able to get through the sky without colliding into each other, all the while climbing steadily. They eventually broke above the storm close to five o'clock and caught dawn's early light. At that point, they moved into their formations. They climbed and leveled off at 10,000 feet and crossed the English Channel, and Jim was able to see the powerful force heading towards France's Normandy coast.

Almost 11,000 airplanes, bombers, and fighters of all types were in the sky that morning. Fighter cover of P-51 Mustangs and Royal Air Force Spitfires escorted them to their target. Below in the Channel, 5,000 ships created a bridge from England to France. Louden had never seen so many ships in his life as that morning when he flew across the Channel.

Their mission that day was to lay 250-pound fragmentation bombs down on Utah Beach at 6:25 a.m., five minutes before the first ground troops were to hit that beach. Both formations had the same target. By successfully laying the bombs, they could knock out the mines and barriers that the Germans had planted in the sand to kill many of the troops when they came ashore. Two miles behind the first formation and 500 feet lower, Louden saw the first box get some mild flak. Thank God, the Germans were so busy defending themselves against the battleships and cruisers in the harbor blasting them, that the flak was ineffective. He anticipated that this treatment awaited his formation's arrival as well.

At 6:25 a.m., they were going down over the target. The last thirty seconds over target, there was no time to take evasive action. No matter how thick the flak was or how close, Jim had to hold the needle ball and air speed.

One could not change a foot of altitude or a degree of heading. Under the clouds and only 3,500 feet above the ground, he had to hold his focus to keep the plane level and on course.

But Jim's adrenalin was flowing that morning, and to this invincible kid, he had a front-row seat to the greatest show of the century. He looked out of the corner of his eye and could see thousands of troops wading ashore from the landing craft coming into Utah Beach.

Omaha Beach was not far away. Utah Beach's losses were minimal, 197 including 60 missing compared to nearly 2,000 casualties at Omaha Beach. In fact, it was not long after D-Day that General Omar Nelson Bradley, commander of the 12th Army Group in Europe, made a comment that Utah Beach was one of the most successful military operations he had ever seen, marked by precision timing. The planes "walked" the bombs down the beach at exactly 6:25 a.m., and the first troops hit the beach at 6:30. The bombs destroyed most of the mines planted in the sand, saving many American and British lives.

After dropping the bombs right on target, Jim's group made a left turn to head back over the English Channel to land and prepare for an immediate second mission. Due to heavy cloud cover, their formation was surprised to find that their return flight took them over Nazi-occupied Jersey Island. Suddenly, black puffs of flak popped up in front of the planes; the Germans were shooting at the noise of the returning planes. With a quick left turn away from danger, the planes headed safely back to Braintree. There was only time to grab a sandwich while the planes refueled and reloaded with 500-pound armor-piercing bombs. Ready to go again, Louden was one of many chosen for round two. With pride and excitement, he prepared his crew.

That afternoon, Jim's squadron, escorted by P-51 Mustangs and RAF Spitfires, bombed inland at a tough target, St. Lo, a well-defended marshalling yard about twenty miles inland from the beachhead. The Germans sent up a lot of flak, but the group hit its target and returned unscathed. It took almost two weeks before St. Lo was captured, because the Germans were so well-solidified there.

In the summer of 1944, Jim flew out of Braintree to bomb a target in northwest Germany. After a successful bombing, the plane headed back to England. The Germans pounded the air with a tremendous amount of flak, and Jim's plane was hit at 10,000 feet, leaving the right engine inoperable.

The B-26 Marauder, with its high wing loading, could do only one thing on one engine – head down. As soon as the engine was lost, Louden pulled out of the formation and yelled to his bombardier-navigator, "Give me a heading to the white cliffs of Dover."

Jim was heading to an emergency strip called Manson, about two miles long and a mile wide on the coast by the white cliffs of Dover. Flying back across the channel, the plane losing altitude all the time, Jim began praying that he would see those white cliffs soon. He ordered his crew to throw everything possible out of the plane, including ammunition and guns, to lighten the load.

Suddenly, off in the distance, maybe forty or fifty miles on the horizon Jim spotted the rugged white cliffs. Fortunately, the Germans were not in pursuit that day, and their plane was protected with fighter protection.

Jim came in from the channel with just a few hundred feet of altitude left, swung in and made a perfect, single-engine landing on the strip amid shouts of relief. His flying suit soaked with perspiration, Jim stepped out of the plane, kissed the ground, and thanked the Good Lord.

"I felt closer to God than I had ever been in my life," he said. "There are no atheists in foxholes or cockpits."

He recalls a popular song from WWII:

Coming In On A Wing and A Prayer

Coming in on a wing and a prayer,
One of our planes was missing, two hours over due.
One of our planes was missing, with all its gallant crew.
The radio sets were humming; they waited for a word;
Then a voice broke thru the humming and this is what they heard:

Chorus

Comin' In On a Wing and A Pray'r
Comin' In On a Wing and A Pray'r
Tho' there's one motor gone, we can still car-ry on,
Com-in' In On A Wing and A Pray'r

What a show, What a fight
Yes, we really hit our tar-get for tonight!
How we sing as we limp thru the air
Look be-low, there's our field over there
With our full crew a-board and our trust in the Lord
We're Comin' In On A Wing and A Pray'r

On December 5, 1944, Jim led a mission through a maze of heavy flak to bomb a bridge close to Cologne. After the successful operation, his squadron commander nominated Jim to receive the Distinguished Flying Cross for outstanding leadership. A few months later, on February 9, 1945, he was promoted to Captain. His nomination for the Distinguished Flying Cross was approved and General Sam Anderson pinned the medal on him in France on February 26, 1945.

The recommendation reads: "First Lieutenant James L. Louden. For extraordinary achievement as pilot of a B-26 aircraft during numerous attacks on important enemy objectives. On December 5, 1944, Lieutenant Louden led his flight through intense anti-aircraft fire to attack the heavily defended Village of Huchem, Germany, with excellent results. Lieutenant Louden's expert airmanship and intrepidity have been of great assistance in carrying the fight to the enemy."

It wasn't long after that Jim's group was transferred from Braintree to Hurn Air Force Base, Bournemouth, England, then over to Ste. Mere Eglise, France, which was not far from Utah Beach. Operations there were performed on a pierced-steel plank runway. Each plank was only twelve inches wide. A large number of them were locked together to fashion a runway 500-feet wide and 4,500-feet long. It was a tough landing, especially during heavy rains, because airplane tires had a tougher time gripping the wet and slippery steel planks than on the typical concrete runways. After two weeks, the 397th was transferred to Dreux Air Force Base, at Chartres, France, about 100 miles southwest of Paris. From there, they flew missions into eastern France and western Germany.

The Germans played the weather card beautifully during the Battle of the Bulge in the Ardennes in December, 1944. They accurately predicted that part of northeastern France and western Germany were going to be socked in by heavy fog. Visibility was less than two feet. For four days,

DISTINGUISHED FLYING CROSS

FIRST LIEUTENANT JAMES L. LOUDEN. FOR EXTRAORDINARY ACHIEVEMENT
AS PILOT OF A B-26 AIRCRAFT DURING NUMEROUS ATTACKS ON IMPORTANT
ENEMY OBJECTIVES. ON 5 DECEMBER 1944, LIEUTENANT LOUDEN LED
HIS FLIGHT THROUGH INTENSE ANTI-AIRCRAFT FIRE TO ATTACK THE
HEAVILY DEFENDED VILLAGE OF HUCHEM, GERMANY WITH EXCELLENT
RESULTS. LIEUTENANT LOUDEN'S EXPERT AIRMANSHIP AND INTREPIDITY
HAVE BEEN OF GREAT ASSISTANCE IN CARRYING THE FIGHT TO THE ENEMY.

Maj. Gen. Anderson honors Jim with his Distinguished Flying Cross on Feb. 26, 1945 in St. Quentin, France.

Allied planes could not take off. In this last-gasp effort of the Germans, the Allied troops were pushed back and thousands of lives were lost.

Once the fog had lifted, heated air action and a counter attack began with Jim's group flying six or seven missions a day. They continuously bombed the Germans as they retreated.

One day, returning from another successful mission, Jim experienced a severe pain in his right side. As it turned out, he was having an acute appendicitis attack in the airplane. His co-pilot took

Maj. Crabtree, left, Cpt. Louden, and Cpt. Neu, right. St, Quentin, France, 1945.

over to land the plane, and they radioed ahead for an ambulance to meet the plane. Jim was rushed to the U.S. military hospital in Chartres, France, where he was operated on the next day. In all of his days of flying, this was the only time he experienced a personal medical emergency in flight.

Having completed fifty missions, Jim figured that after his five-day hospitalization, he would be transferred to a hotel in the country north of London for R & R, and then home to America. But it was early 1945, and the Allies were desperate for pilots to keep pushing the Germans back. Jim was informed that he was going back to combat as soon as he could get on his feet.

Pilot "Big Jim," left of center, with his crew of Blind Date, Dec. 6, 1944.

Within two weeks after his surgery, Jim was back in the cockpit at St. Quentin, France. From there, he flew fourteen more bombing missions over cities and bridges in West Germany. The crew of Blind Date included his co-pilot, Mike Hochella, plus a bombardier, a flight engineer, a gunner, a tail gunner, and a top turret gunner. The crew participated in naming the plane, and a flight engineer painted a nude woman sitting on top of a bomb on the plane's front left fuselage. Blind Date always got them back and was never knocked down.

Jim's friendship with Mike lasted a lifetime until Hochella's death in 2003. A year before, I had a touching experience visiting Mike and his wife, Evelyn, in their home in Allentown, Pennsylvania. They shared wonderful stories about Dad and their WWII squadron. He recounted the story of how Dad had approached Mike to be his co-pilot.

"I didn't hesitate a second in asking my assigned pilot if I could make the switch," Hochella said. "Jim and I flew a lot of missions, and he let me take the controls often. I felt as safe as anyone could feel, flying into combat with 'Big Jim.' It was an honor to fly with him." Mike also remembers how much Dad loved playing the harmonica, often entertaining the squadron on nights they didn't have a flying mission the next morning. These came to be known as "hubba dubba" parties with a little champagne and singing, and Dad was dubbed the "Hubba Dubba Man." As the athletic and recreation officer and public information officer of the squadron, he kept the morale going with his tunes and positive attitude.

The "Hubba Dubba Man" performing with a passion.

To this day, Jim plays to bring joy and uplift people's spirits at the bomb group's annual reunions, and every chance he gets. His two favorite war tunes are *The White Cliffs of Dover*, in honor of his safe landing there, and *Lili Marlene*, in honor of Marlene Dietrich, the german-born actress who denounced Hitler and became a symbol for the Allied Troops.

Jim's lifelong love of music prompted him to use all his influence to talk his squadron commander into a couple of days leave to go see his

45

favorite band leader, Major Glenn Miller. Miller was to lead his band at the USO show on the Champs Elysees in downtown Paris. Jim took a train from St. Quentin into Paris and was in the theater that night, December 15, 1944, with several hundred other GIs — men and women alike waiting for the show to start.

Unannounced, Glenn Miller's drummer, Ray McKinley, walked out onto the stage and made the shocking statement, "I've got something sad to tell you ladies and gentlemen. Glenn Miller took off early this morning from an airbase in Southern England, and he hasn't been found."

Dad said you could hear a pin drop in the packed room as the reality set in that Glenn Miller was gone. Yet, through his legendary music, this great man would live on in everyone's hearts and minds.

Eventually, Jim spoke with several pilots stationed at the airbase where Miller's plane, a light twin-engine utility airplane, had taken off in turbulent weather. The pilots believed that Miller should never have flown that day, but the heroic bandleader was reluctant to disappoint the troops waiting for him in Paris. To this day, Miller's plane has not been found.

The Allied troops walked into Berlin early in May 1945. On May 8, 1945, Germany surrendered unconditionally, and it was all over.

Jim's last mission before heading home in early April, and just before the war officially ended, was more or less a milk run. It was over West Germany to knock out a bridge. The bridge was destroyed with only mild flak and his plane returned to St. Quentin. He felt fortunate that in his sixty-four missions, he never had one crewman injured, although holes from flak pockmarked the planes.

Returning stateside, Jim's first stop was back to Pittsburgh to visit his parents and sister... and to pursue Peggy, the girl who had captured his heart.

Jim and his younger sister Jean.

After a brief 10 days in Pittsburgh, Jim was off to the Don CeSar Hotel, which had been converted by the Army Air Corps to an R & R (rest & recuperation) facility in St. Petersburg, Florida. Ironically, after 64 safe missions in World War II battle zones, Louden was felled on the home front. His stay at the Don CeSar was prolonged after breaking his left arm while playing baseball.

Yes, Jim still loved baseball, and that October he decided to attend the World Series in Chicago. He traveled by train, riding in coach, from Pittsburgh to Chicago and settled in at the Chicago YMCA in hopes of attending the series between the Chicago Cubs and the Detroit Tigers. Like all returning WWII heroes, Jim received all kinds of attention and gracious treatment. Waiting in full uniform to catch a bus to the stadium, Jim was approached by a well-dressed man in a business suit who struck up a conversation.

Upon hearing Jim's story about his love of baseball and his recent service in Europe, the gentleman invited Jim to be his guest at the first two games in his box seats at Wrigley Field. He also insisted that Jim stay at a hotel and paid the tab as a gesture of gratitude. The series went the full seven games, and Detroit won. That was the last time the Cubs appeared in a World Series; if the Cubs ever make it to the World Series again, Jim will no doubt have a front-row seat at Wrigley Field.

The war years made Dad appreciate America all the more. It also fueled his appetite for more flying. He became a civilian when his terminal leave expired on November 15, 1945, but stayed in the reserves to keep flying. Every time he saw an airplane, he wished he was the pilot flying it.

POST WORLD WAR II MILITARY LIFE

*"When one door closes, another opens; but we often look so long
and so regretfully upon the closed door that we do not see
the one that has opened for us."*

— Alexander Graham Bell

Just a month after Dad was honorably discharged, my parents were married on December 15, 1945.

With all the GIs returning home, housing was in short supply, and the happy couple, Jim and Peggy Louden, moved in with my mom's parents in Pittsburgh.

Mom kept working for Rexall Drug, and Dad was back doing what he did before he enlisted: selling meat by the carload for the St. Louis Independent Packing Company to all the butcher shops in Pittsburgh.

In the 1940s, Americans still purchased their food in the European fashion by visiting various specialty shops: bakeries and butcher and cheese shops. Or they had it delivered to their homes. These were the days of the milkman, the bakery wagon, and the Fuller Brush man. Supermarkets wouldn't arrive on the scene until the mid-1950s.

Dad would call on the butcher shops every day, secure the orders, and airmail them nightly from the Pittsburgh airport. Five days later, refrigerated cars of meat would dock at the railroad yard, then trucks would be loaded with the meat to deliver to the butchers.

Dad's new job afforded him the opportunity to meet new friends and discover his natural people skills. He loved being around others and giving them cause to smile and laugh. People trusted Jim Louden; they liked doing business with him. In November of 1945, he attended a sales training workshop in Chicago where he learned the tricks of the trade.

The "Hubba Dubba Man" with his sales training buddies. L&L Café, Chicago, Nov. 1945.

He was indeed good at it, but his heart didn't hold much passion for meat. If he was out walking with Peggy and spotted an Army Air Corps pilot, he would be filled with envy.

"I should be wearing that uniform," he told Peggy time and time again. "I was meant to fly, not sell meat."

He had been in the clouds, viewed the far horizon, and gotten that adrenalin rush each time he dared to fly through flak to score a direct hit on his target. Dad would relive those moments as he shared his stories with Peggy.

"As soon as I'd hear that 'bombs away' call, I'd veer left and get the hell out of there," he'd tell her, using his arm to illustrate the intensity of the move.

But Peggy could only shudder. How could she keep her man down on the ground after he'd soared in the heavens above?

Didn't he understand how dangerous flying was? Why, airplanes had only been invented some forty years ago! Didn't he realize how many of his friends had died in plane crashes? And she had heard the stories of his near calamities. Oh, yes, Peggy knew that Jim had more than a bit of the daredevil in him; she witnessed that increasing sense of invincibility that came with each "mission completed" chalk mark, with every award, every "atta-boy." She read between the lines of every letter he had sent home that this mistress of flight had grabbed hold of her man and would never let go. But she had prayed that Jim would make it home, that they would be married, that they would have children, and live happily ever after.

Nowhere in her prayers or dreams did she envision Jim returning to the service and her traipsing around the world as a military wife. Why, she had never even left her home state of Pennsylvania!

Aw, but he had returned home; they did get married, and they were building a nest egg, saving while they lived with her parents, both of them working, and Jim building a career as a salesman. And he was such a persuasive chap; he was already making great inroads and building a name for himself.

The more determined Jim was to take wing, the more resolute Peggy became in her position to keep her man firmly planted on the ground.

Mom was overwhelmed at the prospect of constant moving that would be demanded by the military lifestyle. She had traveled very little, and her roots were deeply ingrained in Pittsburgh. She had never lived away from her parents, even after her marriage.

81,000 Take Trick Quiz; 9600 to Become Officers

Army Lauds New System for Selecting Men for Regular Commissions

WASHINGTON, June 24 (UP)—Ninety-six hundred war-seasoned, scientifically-picked soldiers have been selected by the Army from 108,000 applicants for permanent officer's commissions. Only 81,000 were allowed to take the final quiz after a physical examination.

Maj. Gen. Willard S. Paul, War Department chief of personnel and administration, described the system for picking the new Regular Army officers as the best method ever devised by public or private organizations for finding men with leadership ability.

Using a scientifically prepared questionnaire, the Army quizzed 13,000 battle-seasoned officers about their fellow officers' ability. The Army gleaned from this a list of 1000 officers rated by their colleagues as "outstanding," 1000 as "average" and 1000 as "poor."

Replace Old 'IQ' Tests

Then psychiatrists developed from these results sets of model, tricky questions which were put to 81,000 applicants for Regular Army commissions. The good leaders answered them one way, the bad in another.

The questionnaires replaced the old type "IQ" tests which, according to Army psychiatrists, have been relegated to "the backwoods."

Surprised by the heavy flow of applicants for its limited number of Regular Army commissions, the Army devised the new test as part of a three-point program to screen the applicants.

First, Gen. Paul said, 27,000 were found physically ineligible. The other 81,000 were subjected to the scientific questioning, evaluation of their qualifications by officers who served with them in the war, and interviews with a board of officers.

Names Go to Congress

Names of the 9600 men who came out on top will be sent to Congress Friday for approval of their permanent commissions. There will be 600 majors, 2000 captains, 6000 first lieutenants and 1000 second lieutenants.

The Army Air Forces will receive 4000 of the newly commissioned men, with the rest going to ground forces and service forces.

An analysis of the new officer crop showed that the average was country-reared, notably mature and possessed abilities qualifying him to fill a junior executive's position in private industry.

Pittsburgh Press, June 24, 1946.

Just months into their marriage, in February 1946, a letter from the War Department arrived: Would Jim Louden be interested in an opportunity to qualify for a regular commission in the Army Air Forces? Based on his World War II military record, he would be allowed to take a series of qualifying tests that would eliminate the necessity of attending West Point for four years.

Oh, yes, Dad was ready. Mom was not.

She gave it her best shot: "Jim, if they take you back in the Army Air Corps as a pilot and regular officer, I'm not going with you."

Was the marriage over before it began? Jim wasn't sure; he knew he loved her and that she loved him. But was this an ultimatum? Was she saying to him, "If you pursue a career in the military, I'm leaving you; it's over."

Not quite.

"I'm not willing to relocate with you to whatever base they assign you," Peggy told him. "I don't want to go around the world and be the wife of a military pilot."

Jim breathed a little easier. He knew he had to fly again, and he knew that Peggy would be waiting for him, albeit disgruntled with his choice of career. But he was confident that he just needed time to get her to come around to his way of thinking. He'd always been able to get what he wanted, "Seek and ye shall find..."

"Peggy, I've got to fly again," he said. "I'm going to at least apply and see what happens."

And off he went to an Army base at Fort Indiantown Gap, Pennsylvania, for a weeklong battery of mental and physical tests and interviews before a board of officers, colonels, and generals.

The military was able to select from a handsome harvest of applicants in every specialty. The search was for officers whose records demonstrated leadership and the ability to perform effectively in positions of responsibility. Major General Fred Anderson, the Army's chief of personnel, wanted group commanders and officers who had been picked from units and placed in responsible staff positions.

"The individual will be considered outstanding if he is recognized by his superiors and fellow officers as excelling in leadership, moral fiber, integrity, courage, and overall efficiency in whatever task or duty assigned," Anderson decreed. "He must be truly the cream of the crop."

Without specifically stating so, the criteria directed the selection process toward rated officers, mainly pilots, by emphasizing qualities that one expected in combat commanders.

The process included an evaluation of three wartime officer efficiency reports on each applicant, a biographical questionnaire completed by the individual, and an interview conducted by a board of officers. Points were assigned for each part, and total points were tallied to give a composite score. Additional changes were adopted to use the composite score as a guideline with final selection authority vested within each Army branch.

More than 108,000 men applied for the commissions; 81,000 were allowed to take the final test after a physical examination, and only 9,600 war veterans were selected. Their names were sent to Congress for approval of their permanent commissions: There would be 600 majors, 2,000 captains, 6,000 first lieutenants, and 1,000 second lieutenants.

The Army Air Corps would receive 4,000 of the newly commissioned men, with the remainder designated for ground and service forces. Less than four percent of the initial applicants were selected; Jim would not know his fate for months.

After the grueling week, Jim was told to return home and expect a telegram from the War Department the last week of June. For the time being, he was back in the meat business.

When he told Peggy about the timeline, she was unwavering in her position. "I hope that telegram never comes," she told him flatly.

Jim silently began counting the days. And praying.

Sure enough, June 28, 1946, the telegram arrived. "Congratulations! You have been accepted as a regular officer in the United States Army Air Corps."

Jim saw his life laid out before him and was filled with pride. He was to be an officer in the U.S. Army Air Corps. This son of a bricklayer had made it without a college education. He had made it based on the strength of his character and skills demonstrated when his country and the free world needed him. He had soared.

And just as Jim's heart took flight, Peggy's fell. A week later, Second Lieutenant James Louden reported to the A-26 Light Bomber, Night Attack Group, 47th Bomb Group, at Lake Charles, Louisiana. Peggy, true to her word, did not accompany him.

For the next six months, Dad flew a number of missions in the A-26 Douglas Invader Light Bomber and then received orders to report to Tyndall Army Air Corps Base in Panama City, Florida. He was to attend Airtac School for administration training in running a squadron.

But first, he would return to Peggy and Pittsburgh for Christmas. Absence had indeed made the heart grow fonder, and this time Jim was successful in persuading Peggy to join him that spring in Panama City.

Jim found a furnished cottage on a white-sand beach, and Peggy flew down to tropical Florida.

But it wasn't a honeymoon existence; for Peggy, it was more like "The Castaways."

Each day, Jim's flying buddies would pick him up for his eight hours of work, and Peggy was marooned in this new humid environment. The couple didn't own a car, so Peggy wasn't able to meet the other military wives.

Bugs were big in this tropical climate. One night, Peggy walked barefoot into the kitchen, turned on the lights, and dozens of cockroaches scurried for cover. Then she encountered hundreds of flying termites. Jim told her that he would get the landlord to come over and spray, but he was beginning to think this might not have been the best idea after all.

Dad came home one day and found Mom in tears, "I can't take this," she cried. Lonely and frustrated, she confessed she was ready to go back to Pittsburgh.

Mom did return home, but was ready to give it another go, when Dad was transferred two months later to El Paso, Texas. He had learned his lesson in Florida. This time, Dad searched until he found a nice, furnished two-bedroom apartment and also purchased a two-door Mercury.

This time around, things were indeed better for Peggy Louden. Now she had a car, very much her own first set of wings. She had a much finer apartment, and soon she made friends with the other officers' wives. She became good friends, lifelong friends in fact, with Charlotte Chapman, the wife of Col. Willis Chapman, then commander of the 47th Bomb Group.

Not only was Mom evolving into the dutiful officer's wife, she began to thrive in the active, social scene.

"Everybody loved Peggy," Dad told me. "Her goal early in life was to be a Radio City Music Hall Rockette; she even wrote to them when she was twelve-years-old.

"All the guys wanted to dance with Peggy," Dad remembers. "She could polka, rumba, tango, and foxtrot."

Mom even took to the skies herself in El Paso. In 1947, there was a standing rule that a pilot could take his wife up once a year in the A-26 Invader Light Bomber, the plane Dad had been flying on day and night attack mission flight training. Mom sat in the co-pilot seat while Dad flew over the Rio Grande River at 300 miles per hour. She loved it, and for the first time began to understand Dad's ecstasy for the heavens.

Peggy, left, happy at last in Texas.

In that same year, as a result of the National Security Act of September 8, 1947, the United States Army Air Forces became the US Air Force, and was completely separated from the Army. In this act, a division of duties was established that prohibited the Army from operating any fixed wing, jet-powered attack aircraft, or tactical reconnaissance aircraft.

Not surprisingly, Jim and his 47th Bomb Group, stationed at Biggs Field in El Paso, Texas, had a celebration party.

In November 1948, the bomb group received delivery of their first jet bomber, the B-45. The group, all 600 plus their families, was transferred to Barksdale Air Force Base in Shreveport, Louisiana, which afforded a longer runway required by this new jet-propelled aircraft.

Made by North American Aviation, the B-45 was the first operational jet bomber and the first four-jet aircraft to fly in the United Sates. Its four engines were arranged in pairs of wing-mounted nacelles, which proved to be very dangerous. A number of engineering lessons were learned from this bomber, the predecessor to the B-47, B-52, and other large jet bombers subsequently produced over the years.

Dad didn't know it at the time, but his own experiences in the B-45 would one day be among those engineering lessons.

Col. Chapman asked Jim if he would serve as public information officer for the 47th Bomb Group. This was quite an honor for a young captain, particularly because there was strong public interest in the B-45, which along with the new jet fighters would revolutionize United States supremacy in air warfare. Jim would prove to be a natural-born public information officer. After all, this was the "Hubba Dubba Man" who had always built up the morale of his squadron with his upbeat nature and harmonica playing.

Two more B-45s arrived at the Barksdale base. And Jim was about to find himself in a funnel cloud with miracles all around him.

The B-45, America's first operational jet bomber. Biggs Field, El Paso, Texas.

SAVED BY THE TOSS OF A COIN

"As we move through life, we move accompanied. Call it what you will - spirit, energy, angel, being. I call it... The Guardian."

— Patricia Chapman Meder

Thursday, June 9, 1949 was a first-class day to fly at Barksdale Air Force Base. Beautiful morning, gentle wind, and not a cloud in the sky. It would be the third time Jim Louden had gone up in the B-45.

As public information officer for the first jet bomber group in the history of the United States Air Force, Capt. Louden had coordinated a contest the previous year to name the aircraft. The name "Tornado" was chosen.

Tornados are also known as twisters; it was a fortuitous choice.

The first two times Jim had flown in the B-45 Tornado he made radio broadcasts from the plane's cockpit. Jim's broadcasts, which captured the impressions of a pilot flying a B-45 at 45,000 feet, were radioed to the local NBC station in Shreveport and relayed nationwide from there.

The B-45 featured a tandem cockpit: the front for the pilot, the rear for the co-pilot. On his first two flights, Jim sat in the rear behind the instructor pilot who was flying the plane.

But today, Jim and Capt. Ralph Smith would learn to fly the B-45 Tornado, under the tutelage of Instructor Pilot Capt. Milton Costello.

Jim had flown the B-26 Martin Marauder on 64 missions in World War II. But the B-45 Tornado was another kind of plane entirely, and he was looking forward to getting to know how this beauty handled.

Jim had survived one harrowing mission when his B-26 got hit by flak, lost an engine, and made it back on a wing and a prayer to the emergency-landing strip near the white cliffs of Dover. Jim had survived that turbulent night to fly on this quiet, sunny day, back in the good old USA where the only flak he encountered was occasional radio static.

The three pilots met at 0-900 and were looking forward to a few hours where each would practice putting the B-45 7033 in a stall and pulling out of it again, practicing landings and take-offs through a series of "touch-and-go" exercises, and just getting the general feel of the airplane.

Costello asked who would fly the first two hours, while the other student would sit in the nose of the plane, at the navigator's position, awaiting his turn at the controls. Smith and Louden looked at each other and shrugged, so Costello pulled out a dime for a coin toss.

Louden called heads and lost.

"I'll teach Smitty how to land this thing and give him some single-engine work at altitude," Costello said. "Then you guys will switch seats."

With an "Okay by me," Jim crawled into the nose, donned his crash helmet and backpack parachute, and strapped himself in, separated from his buddies by a five-inch firewall.

In actuality, Jim Louden won the toss; two hours later, he was alive. By sitting in the nose, rather than the cockpit, he had survived the U.S. Air Force's first fatal crash of a B-45 in 1949.

At approximately 10:20 a.m., Costello secured permission from the Barksdale tower to bring the plane in for a touch-and-go on runway 14. The plane was coming in on final approach, wing flaps down as normal. At 2,000 feet, the plane suddenly dipped. Costello instinctively tried to pull up the wing by applying full power to all four engines.

Completely out of control and two-and-a-half miles short of the runway, the plane smashed into the ground and 16,000 pounds of jet fuel exploded on impact.

As noted by Peggy— "This is where they found Jim. They claim those trees helped to save his life." — photo compliments of Shreveport Journal. June 9, 1949

Only Big Jim and the tail survived. — photo compliments of Shreveport Journal. June 9, 1949

RESTRICTED

STATEMENT STATEMENT STATEMENT

15 June, 1949

At approximately 08:30 hours the pilots arrived and made their pre-flight inspection. The A/C was accepted for flight at approximately 08:50 hours. At approximately 09:00 hours, engines were started, and at approximately 09:10 hours the A/c was taxied out from the parking area.

[signature]
Hendrickson, Mendal E. M/Sgt. A.F.

[signature]
Brown, William A. S/Sgt. A.F.

[signature]
Coleman, John E. Jr. S/Sgt. A.F.

I, Thomas J. Williams, 1st Lt., AO-691200, was tower officer on the date of this crash.

I heard B-45 7033 call in for an approach and go-around. I saw 7033 on the downwind leg for landing on on runway 140, then, due to heavy traffic, my attention was diverted elsewhere.

Over the VHF radio, at approximately 1022 came a frenzied transmission, "go around" - immediately after this, a transmission, hysterical, screaming, "take it around." I looked around for T-6, thinking one of them was in trouble, I saw this B-45 in a diving turn to the left about two and one half (2 1/2) miles northeast of the field at approximately 150-200 feet. He was turning toward a southerly heading. At about fifty or seventy five feet, he leveled his wings and pulled his nose up into what appeared to be level flight. The aircraft however, mushed into the ground in this attitude. Immediately after this, a terrific billowing explosion ensued.
Then, the aircraft began burning.

Crashed aircraft procedure followed.

[signature]
Williams, Thomas J. 1st Lt., AO-691200

RESTRICTED

STATEMENT STATEMENT STATEMENT

I, Thomas B. Catron, 1st Lt., A0-27770, 3500th Pilot
Training Wing, at approximately 1020 hours, 9 June 1949,
was in the rear cockpit of a T-6 flying locally out of
Barksdale Air Force Base for the purpose of giving transi-
tion to another instructor. As we turned onto the base
leg preparatory to landing on runway 14, I looked back
and saw a B-45 at approximately 1200 ft. indicated in a
moderate right turn coming from the south between my ship
and the field wiht his gear down. I lowered the nose and
continued my turn, and then looked back down. I lowered
the nose and continued my turn,, and then looked back to
make certain I was clear of the B-45. At first, I was
unable to locate it, but finally I saw it down close to
the ground in what seemed to be a 20 degree diving angle
and a 30 degree bank to the right. As I watched, he
continued down at an airspeed definitely above stalling
speed until he crashed into a field approximately 3 miles
northeast of the northwest end of runway 32 right.

Subject B-45 began coming apart and burning within one
or two seconds after impact. I notified the tower of the
crash and circled the scene of the accident until crash
equipment arrived.

_____
Catron, Thomas B. 1st Lt., A0-27770

On 9 June 1949, this officer was giving a T-6 check out to
Captain MacCauley. At approximately 10:20 while on the down
wind leg for a landing on runway 14 east, I heard the order
given "take it around," on channel "F" VHF. Immediately
after this we turned onto the base leg, and just before
turning onto the final, I heard a voice shout "bail
out, bail out, bail out," over the same VHF channel.

I looked for an aircraft in an emergency during the final
turn, and as we rolled out, I saw an unidentified aircraft
crash and explode approximately 4 miles east of the field.

Captain MacCauley was not monitoring Channel "F" and did
not hear any of the foregoing. After I called his attention
to the crash, we pulled up and circled directing the crash
trucks to the accident through the tower untill they
reached the scene.

_____
Kersey, Maurice M. 1st Lt., A0-804455

—photo compliments of Shreveport Journal, June 9, 1949.

—photo compliments of Shreveport Journal, June 9, 1949.

The B-45 ploughed across an alfalfa field leaving in its wake its tail assembly, a jet engine, and the twisted fuselage, and piling up other debris as it approached little Alligator Bayou, about 150 yards from where it first struck ground.

Fragments were found strewn along the field; other parts were found in a swampy stand of trees and still more in a field beyond the trees.

Burning fuel and oil from the wreckage was visible from downtown Shreveport, nine miles away. It was still burning fiercely two hours after the crash, despite the efforts of crash and fire crews from Barksdale Air Force Base.

Jim Sharpe, a young Air Force supply sergeant, happened to be outside when the plane went down. At age 19, he had never been in war and had never experienced something so devastating in his life. He never forgot it. For years, he wondered what had happened to the survivor. He continued to search for Jim only to locate and meet him for the first time years later in 1996.

"What a thrill to talk to a man who had not only survived that incredible day, but had gone on to live such an active and fulfilled life."

Sharpe described the scene.

"We grabbed can and hauled buggy around the base to get there just 30 minutes after the ambulance had taken Jim to the hospital," said Sharpe. "We didn't expect to find anyone alive; there was fire everywhere, and there wasn't enough of that plane to even recognize it. I'd never experienced war, and this was the worst scene I had ever laid my eyes on.

"I spotted a busted up helmet beneath a clump of trees. I hesitantly rolled it over, with an almost eerie expectation that I would find the remains of a human skull."

The Weather

(United States Weather Bureau.)
Shreveport and Vicinity—Partly cloudy to cloudy this afternoon, tonight and Friday with local thundershowers. Highest temperature this afternoon about 92; lowest tonight near 70. Sun rises Friday at 5:07, sets at 7:22.

Shreveport Jo

2 DIE IN JET BOMI

Third Ma
Seriously
Injured

Accident Occu
Within Sight O

Two men w
and a third se
ured about 1
Thursday whe
four-engined je
attached to
seventh bomb
Barksdale Air

FRIDAY, JUNE 10, 1949

Pittsburgher Hurt
In Jet Plane Crash

Brentwood War Ace
Is Lone Survivor

A Pittsburgh air hero was in critical condition today after the crash of a jet bomber near Barksdale Field, La.

Capt. James L. Louden, 28, of 0 W. Garden Rd., Brentwood, was the only survivor after a -45 bomber plunged into a hill-side in a landing approach. The four-engine bomber, capable of speeds up to 500 miles an hour, burst into flames immediately.

'Bridge Buster' Group

Capt. Louden served as a flight commander with a B-26 "Bridge Buster" group in World War II. He was awarded the Distinguished Flying Cross for leading his flight through heavy enemy opposition to carry out assignments during the Normandy invasion.

He left the University of Pittsburgh to enter the Air Corps.

CAPT. JAMES L. LOUDEN
Pittsburgher hurt in crash.

Crash Victim
Still Critical

Capt. James L. Lou cally injured in a B-45 jet bo crash here last Thursday, w ported "improved" last nigh the public information offic Barksdale Air Force base.

Although the Captain recog his wife, who came here Pittsburgh, Pa., Barksdale au ties said his condition could be termed as critical. He has in a coma since the time of t cident and has regained cons ness only for brief intervals.

Captain Louden, whose ho in Pittsburgh, is public rela officer for the 47th bombard

Clippings taken from Shreveport Journal & Pittsburgh Press, 1949.

FOUR SECTIONS
40 PAGES

Thursday Afternoon
June 9, 1949

Vol. 54 • Price 5 Cents

CRASH

ight Chance
or Pilot Here

pt. James L. Louden, 28, of
'est Garden Rd., Brentwood,
given only slight chance of
very today from injuries he

ESTERN
UNION

BUX FORT GEORGE G MEADE JUNE 9 1949 467PM

PTAIN JAMES L LOUDEN IS SERIOUSLY ILL STATION HOSPITAL
TO AIRPLANE CRASH NINTH OF JUNE 1949 PD RECOMMEND

NDING OFFICER BARKSDALE AIRBASE SHREVEPORT LOUISIANA

ECIATE SUGGESTIONS FROM ITS PATRONS CONCERNING ITS SERVICE

ash Survivor
ay Be Moved

apt. James Louden, public in-
mation officer of the 47th bomb
g, may be removed to a genera.
ital for treatment for injuries
ived in the crash of a B-45 jet
ber near Barksdale Air Force
e two weeks ago.

Louden Recovering

June 31 – Times

Capt. James L. Louden, air force
officer who survived a jet plane
crash near Barksdale Air Force
base recently, is expected to re-
cover fully, it was announced
yesterday.

His physician at the base hos-
as pro-
l may
a gen-
treated
sion.
to his

Plucky Jim— Sept 15, 1949

Capt. JAMES L. LOUDEN,
who narrowly escaped death
when a B-45 jet bomber crashed
two months ago, was back at
Barksdale air force base this
week on a visit.

As it turned out, the helmet was Jim's. He had been thrown – or blown – from the plane and hurled 125 yards through a barbed-wire fence and into the trees.

The fence tore through his flesh. His teeth were smashed. But the trees cushioned him from the intensity of his fall. He was bleeding profusely and sustained first and second-degree burns. An arm and an ankle were broken. His flight helmet was split down the middle. His vertebrae were cracked. He had a severe concussion and was unconscious.

But, he was alive. Being in the cockpit, Costello and Smith remained with the plane as it crashed. We honor them as the unsung heroes of that day.

Someone found Jim hanging from those tree limbs; his own limbs crushed and broken. He would live to see another day. It would be some years before he would learn about a young rescuer by the name of Ned Touchstone.

Touch-And-Go

For seventeen days, Jim lay in critical condition and was not expected to live.

He was experiencing his own touch-and-go episodes, drifting in and out of consciousness, dancing and flirting with life hereafter, as the doctors held a grave prognosis for his recovery.

Peggy, who had been visiting her mother and father in Pittsburgh, Pennsylvania, received a telephone call from Col. Chapman who had to break the bad news. It was the Army's standard operating procedure to notify next of kin via telegram. Just hours after the colonel's call, Peggy received the official telegram from Fort Meade, Maryland, informing her of her husband's crash and recommending her immediate presence.

Col. Chapman's daughter, Pat Chapman Meder, recalled to me that her dad had said Mom took it surprisingly well.

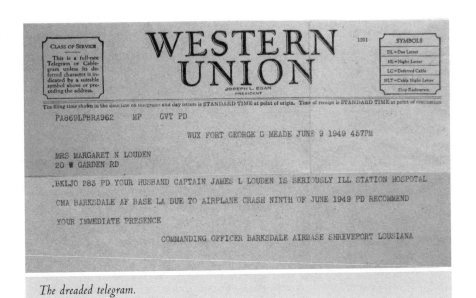

The dreaded telegram.

"Through those early days of life or death uncertainty and during Jim's long road to recovery – Dad described Peggy as remaining strong as a brick," said Pat. "Peggy came that same day to our house and stayed with us for a couple of days. Dad and Mom were two of her primary supporters. Dad said that many people came to see her often and that she handled it beautifully."

Peggy then went to stay with her good friend Marge Kaufmann until the accident investigation was completed.

For days on end, Peggy sat alone with her unconscious husband, praying, wondering, and envisioning outcomes. Should she pray for Jim's recovery? Or would it be kinder to let him go? Would he have brain damage? Should she have tried harder to talk him out of flying? What would she do without him?

There was one particular incident that concerned Peggy and the physicians regarding Jim's mental capacities. The Commander of Training Command, a Four-Star General, visited Jim daily the first few days. As he vacillated between sleep and semi-consciousness, Jim kept insisting that the General was "Mugsy" John McGraw, the former New York Giants manager who had finally arrived to sign him to a big-league baseball contract. His love of baseball, first and foremost on his mind, perhaps helped give him the hope he needed to survive.

Two-and-a-half weeks later, Jim awoke to find Peggy sitting by his bed. He remembered nothing about the crash.

"I'm sure I heard it all, because I was listening to the radio," he said. "But the last thing I remember is the tower saying, 'You're cleared number one to land on runway 14.'"

He was lying in Barksdale's station hospital with his left leg and left arm in traction, suffering from severe internal injuries, severe shock, first and second-degree burns, and multiple lacerations about the head and body.

Marge Kaufmann recalls that Peggy had become her best friend when she, herself, was a young bride and new to the military way of life. She and her husband, Len, were home on leave when the crash occurred, and they immediately drove back to Barksdale to be of help in any way.

"Peggy was so alone," Marge said. "Jim had always been the strong one, the natural-born ham who made life appear so easy. Now Peggy would have to be strong for Jim. And it was up to us, her Air Force family, to close ranks around her and comfort her."

Jim could not be moved for a month and was then transferred to the Army Navy General Hospital in Hot Springs, Arkansas, for further treatment that spanned another five months. A full body cast was part of his treatment. He said it itched him so bad that he would have Mom scratch his back under the cast with a long wire coat hanger.

Smiling his way to recovery,
Hot Springs, Arkansas.
—photo by Marge Kaufmann

"For the first month at Barksdale, they couldn't think about moving me," Jim said. "But once they did air-vac me to Hot Springs, they started me on a physical therapy regimen and electrical stimulation of my left arm, which had been hurriedly reset at the time of the accident. Calcium had formed around the ulna nerve, causing me to have a drop wrist and leaving me with no use of my left arm."

An orthopedic physician wanted to do exploratory surgery.

One of the hospital's physical therapists, an Army Captain, raised a red flag, strongly but quietly advising Jim to request a transfer to Walter Reed Army Medical Center in Washington D.C., where more highly qualified neurosurgeons could more accurately diagnose his injuries. They could then recommend whether or not an operation was required or, if over time, the nerve injury would gradually heal. Evidently, some nerve injuries can heal without surgery — naturally, but slowly, about one inch a month.

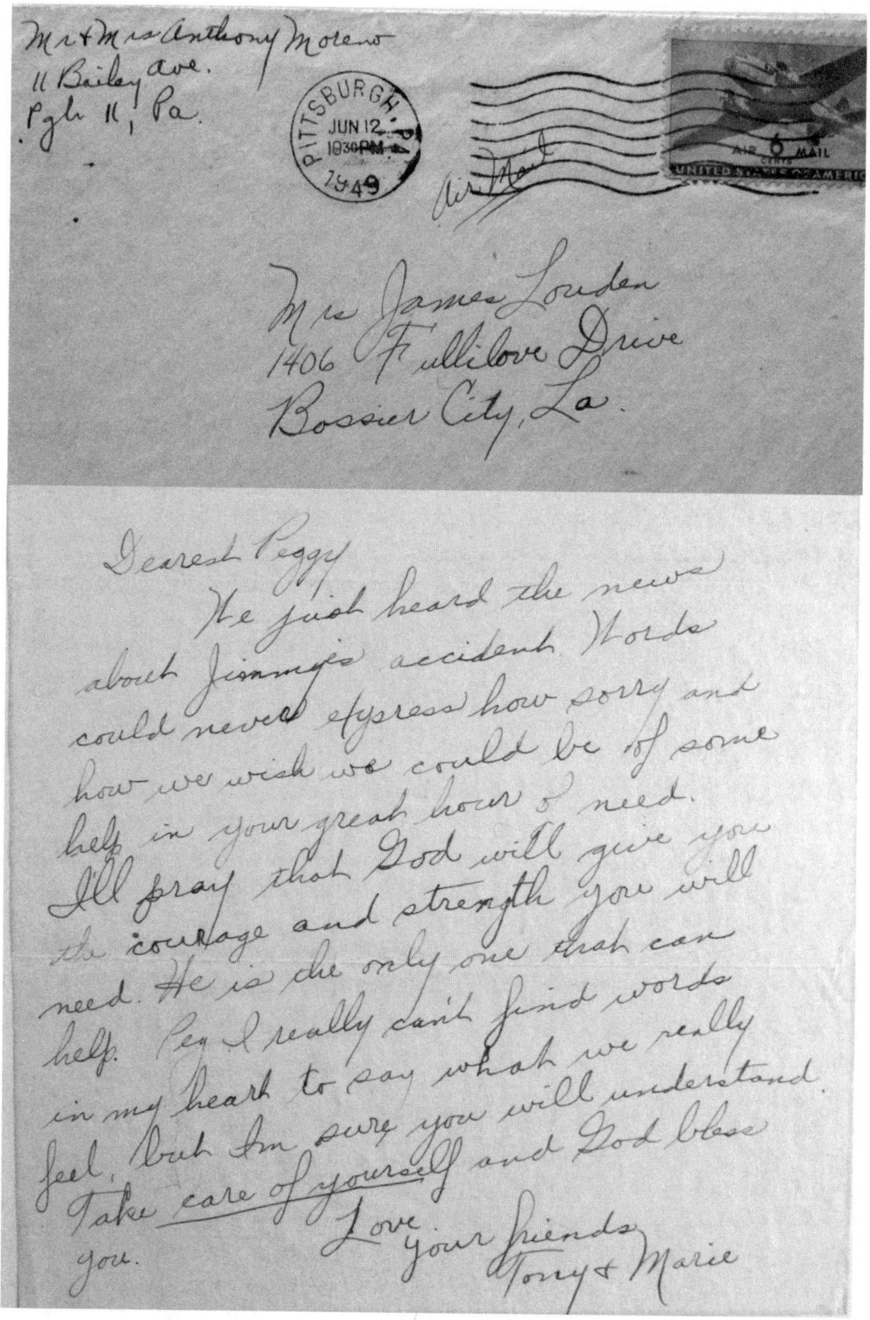

Mr & Mrs Anthony Moreno
11 Bailey Ave.
Pgh 11, Pa.

PITTSBURGH, PA. JUN 12 1030 PM 1949

AIR 6 MAIL UNITED STATES OF AMERICA

Air Mail

Mrs James Louden
1406 Fullilove Drive
Bossier City, La.

Dearest Peggy

We just heard the news about Jimmy's accident. Words could never express how sorry and how we wish we could be of some help in your great hour of need. I'll pray that God will give you the courage and strength you will need. He is the only one that can help. Peg I really can't find words in my heart to say what we really feel, but I'm sure you will understand. Take care of yourself and God bless you.

Love
Your friends
Tony & Marie

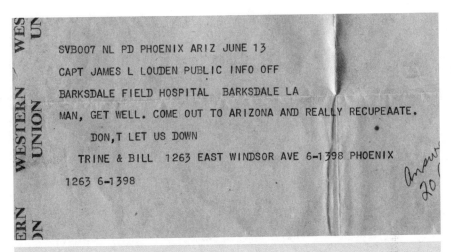

SVB007 NL PD PHOENIX ARIZ JUNE 13

CAPT JAMES L LOUDEN PUBLIC INFO OFF

BARKSDALE FIELD HOSPITAL BARKSDALE LA

MAN, GET WELL. COME OUT TO ARIZONA AND REALLY RECUPEAATE.

    DON,T LET US DOWN

    TRINE & BILL 1263 EAST WINDSOR AVE 6-1398 PHOENIX

    1263 6-1398

Encouraging letters and telegrams from friends.

"Exploratory surgery could cause this to be a permanent injury," she cautioned him, "and if that happens, you'll never be able to fly again, you know."

Jim heard her loud and clear and listened to the message from this angel advisor.

"I knew I needed to get to Walter Reed, and I went to see the hospital commander that day," Jim recalled. "But I had to be careful about how I presented my request, never raising an issue over their quality of care. That would mean automatic denial. I innocently explained that it was difficult for my parents to make repeated trips down to Arkansas to visit me; Walter Reed would be much more convenient for my family."

"Request granted, Louden."

9/ 9/2003   FILE COPY, VARO, WSNC

CLINICAL RECORD BRIEF	a. Hosp STA HOSP BARᴋSDALE AFB LA.		1. Last Name, First Nam Middle Initial Louden, Jame. ᴸ.			
	b. Ward 7	c. Religion P	d. Prev. Adm. No	2. Register No. 55 769	3. Army Serial No. AO 37 710	4. Grade Capt.
	e. Name and Address of Nearest Relative Mrs Margaret L. Louden 1406 Fullilove (W) Bossier City, Louisiana		5. Organization and Arm or Service (if AAF personnel, see below)* USAF Hq & Hq Sq 47th Bomb Wg. (Plt)		
			6. Age 28	7. Race W	8. Length of Service 7	9. Date of Admission 9 June 49
	f. Dis.	Inj. I	B/C	g. Admitting Officer Lt Col W/o	10. Source of Admission Direct	
	* If AAF, indicate pilot, non-pilot flying personnel, ground personnel or aviation cadet.				

11. Final Diagnosis, Additional Diagnoses, Operations, Change of Status

1045

1. Fracture, humerus, upper one-third, left, complete, simple.
2. Fracture, fibula, upper one-third, left, complete, simple.
3. Fracture, ribs, 7, 8, 9, 10, complete, simple.
4. Wound, lacerated and contused, legs, anterior aspect, upper one-third, severe.
5. Burns, 1st and 2nd degree, leg, arm and forearm, right, moderate.
6, Concussion, severe.

1, 2, 3, 4, 5 & 6, AI in airplane crash, while officer was on duty, 3 miles east of Barksdale AF Base, La., 9 June 1949.

	PROFILE				SERIAL				
	P	U	L	H	E	S	X	R	D
Last (if known)	1	1	1	1	1	1	1		
Present									

12. Line of Duty 1, 2, 3, 4, 5 & 6, Yes	13. Disposition and Date Trfd Army & Navy Gen Hosp, Hot Springs, Ark. 6 July 1949	14. Signature of Ward Surgeon /s/ Robert D. Whittington, Jr., Lt Col., MC

WD AGO FORM 1 APR 1945   8-33   ☆ U. S. GOVERNMENT PRINTING OFFICE 16—40778-1   Replaces WD AGO Form 8-33, 1 Jul 44 and WD MD Form 55A, 31 May 39, which are obsolete.

Jim's VA record confirms the severity of his injuries.

The Long Road to Recovery

The road to recovery was to be one long, tough haul that tested my dad's physical, mental, spiritual, and emotional forte every step of the way. His treatments included daily electrical stimulation and grueling, monotonous physical therapy.

Dad moved his hands in occupational therapy by making rugs and salt and pepper shakers. I remember these things in our closets. I always wondered about them; why weren't they used? But now I can see that Mom must have kept them around as mementos of what they had been through, and equally as important, how they had survived and moved on.

I asked my dad, as I wrestled with my own physical trauma, what allowed him to handle the uncertainty about his future career, as well as the severe pain and immobility? How could this athletic man cope with immobility?

He told me that he focused all his attention on healing, showing gratitude to the nurses who took such good care of him, and accepting whatever path he was facing. By keeping actively busy and committed to his healing, his positive mental attitude kept him going through the challenges.

"Teri, all I can say is that I focused all my attention on getting better, and I prayed continuously," Dad said. "And it was important for me to let my nurses know how grateful I was to them; they took such good care of me.

"And I knew I would get better. But whatever path I faced, I would accept. I would keep busy and stay committed," Dad said. "The Good Lord would look out for me; things would work out just fine. I always knew that."

cJAVED BY THE TOSS OF A COIN

And how, dear Dad, could you cope with the risks you took every time you went up in so many different aircraft over the years? Dad didn't hesitate a second to rattle off his answers. They appeared deceivingly simple:

★ *Be proud versus scared.*

★ *Believe that God has a plan for you.*

★ *Realize you have nothing to fear but fear itself.*

★ *Let fear be your best friend.*

★ *Know that when your time has come, it has come.*

Amazingly, Dad's answers shed insight not only on flying, but also served as analogies to living life fully with no regrets. One thing is for certain; despite the risks Dad faced, he not only survived, he remains an active, happy and spirited man, even now, well into his eighties.

"There were four miracles that allowed me to survive my B-45 crash and pointed me back to the skies above," Jim says. "I lost a coin toss. I was blown into a plot of trees that provided cushioning to an otherwise fatal fall. An angel, an Army Captain who was my physical therapist, pointed me northward to Walter Reed. And many years later I learned that I had been touched by another angel, this one in the form of a young man who brought me back from certain death."

Ned Touchstone, an up and coming newspaper editor at just 22-years-old, was visiting his father at his boyhood home near Barksdale, Louisiana. As father and son stood in the yard talking, they heard a loud explosion and saw smoke rising beyond a thin line of woods no more than two miles away.

Both knew right away it was a plane crash, and they made a beeline in the family sedan for the site.

On the scene, Ned saw two bodies, obviously deceased, burning amid the wreckage, with fragments of the plane scattered throughout the alfalfa fields. But Ned believed there might be other survivors.

"How many crew does this plane carry?" he called out. Another rescuer asserted that the B-45 could carry 11 or 12 people. It was actually designed for four.

Ned sprinted across the open field following the debris trail into the trees. "I remember jumping a barbed-wire fence," Ned later reported. "I don't know how I did it. I could not do it before or since." In the trees, he found an unconscious Jim Louden bleeding profusely.

"He was drowning in his own blood," Ned said. "I pulled his tongue free so he wouldn't choke. Then I took off my t-shirt and used it as a tourniquet on his left arm."

Jim wasn't aware of Ned's role in his rescue until 11 years later in 1960 when a letter arrived.

Ned, now working as an aide to a Louisiana Congressman who was chair of the House Armed Services Committee, had replayed the crash scene over and over in his mind for years, always wondering if the man he found in the trees had survived. Now, his work with the Congressman pointed him in the direction of an answer: Ned wrote a letter of inquiry and sent it to the Pentagon, which located Jim Louden at Lockbourne Air Force Base near Columbus, Ohio, and forwarded Touchstone's letter.

Its arrival was quite a shock to Jim, who assumed that air rescue had saved him. He sent a letter of thanks back to Touchstone, but then life moved on as he left for his new assignment in Izmir, Turkey. It was the last contact he would have with Ned for 28 years.

As always, life had pulled Jim Louden ever forward. He and Mom put the crash behind them, and it was not a point of discussion in our family when I was growing up. Dad eventually lost Ned's letter, but he never forgot what Ned had done. "If this young man had not come along on the scene, I would have died; I have no doubt of that," he said.

Thus, in May of 1988, when Jim's friend, Retired Air Force Col. Ted Jakubowski announced he was traveling to Shreveport, the men conversed and a plan was hatched.

"When I get down there, I'm going to the site of the crash," Jakubowski vowed. "And when I go to Barksdale's officers' club, I'll drink a scotch to the one who got away — Jim Louden."

Jim asked him to do something else. Could he try and find the man who had saved his life, the man whose name had been lost long ago?

Ted promised he would.

It turned out to be a tough job. Jakubowski sorted through the Shreveport newspaper, but the archives were limited. Then he contacted Tom Ostendorf, a Shreveport stockbroker and the father of his son's roommate at the Naval Academy. Ostendorf began his own investigation, checking with the 8th Air Force Historical Office. It had details of the crash, but no names of rescuers. But Ostendorf was given the name of a person who might have been involved, a fellow who owned a taxidermy shop not far from the north end of the Barksdale runway. Seems the man had lived there his entire life, Ostendorf was advised.

Jakubowski made a series of phones calls and eventually reached a local bookstore owner, the son of the taxidermist. He had reached out and touched Ned Touchstone. Ned could not believe that after 39 years, Jim Louden was trying to locate him.

Ned closed his bookstore that day and took Jakubowski around the corner to eat shrimp, drink beer, and talk about the thing that had brought two strangers, Ned and Ted, together. They toasted their lives, the pilots whose lives were lost, and the life that had been saved.

"There is one request you can pass on to Jim for me," Ned said glibly. "Tell him he owes me a t-shirt."

Later that day, Touchstone and Louden spoke to each other for the first time. They talked about how two lives had intersected on a fateful day, about bravery beyond duty, about how one man's life was saved, and how two children had come into the world as a result. Emotion traveled over the lines, voices cracked, and eyes traveled into a distant past; two men in the twilights of their careers were once again young. And both were grateful their paths had crossed so long ago and again today. They made plans to meet that summer.

In the meantime, Jim Louden made good on his IOU of one t-shirt. He mailed Ned Touchstone a fine one, inscribed with the date of the crash and the words, "Ned Touchstone, thanks to your heroic deed that day, I am able to replace the shirt you took off your back to save my life. Forever grateful, Jim Louden."

Jim mailed the shirt just prior to Memorial Day, 1988, and had travel arrangements made for his Touchstone reunion. But it was not to come to pass; Ned passed away just weeks later. But Jim knows there will be a reunion someday... just beyond the clouds.

9 JUNE 1949 - B45 CRASH,
BARKSDALE AFB, LA.

NED TOUCHSTONE, THANKS
TO YOUR HEROIC DEED THAT
DAY, I'M ABLE TO REPLACE THE
SHIRT THAT YOU TOOK OFF YOUR
BACK TO SAVE MY LIFE.

FOREVER GRATEFUL,

LT/COL, USAF (RET)
FAYETTEVILLE, N.C.
29 APRIL 1988

Forever grateful to Ned Touchstone.   *— photo by Cindy Burnham, Fayetteville Observer*

Crash Recap

So, what did happen that caused the crash of the B-45 Tornado that hot June day?

In an effort to determine the cause of the accident that took the lives of two pilots, a seven-man board of officers conducted a full-scale probe of the crash.

This B-45 crash was the first ever to have every piece of the plane brought back and laid out in a hangar exactly as the pieces were found. This was ordered by Col. Chapman, commander of the 47th Bomb Group, whose intent was to learn as much as possible about the crash and prevent future mechanical errors. Today, this is a common practice in the aviation world— both military and commercial. Col. Chapman had the distinction of being the only Commander of the 47th Bomb Group during the first four hectic years while the B-45 was being launched.

Through this careful investigation, it was determined that the torque tube on the right flap broke, causing the right flap to come up while the left flap stayed down. And with one flap up and another down and the pilot trying to correct with full power, the B-45 Tornado did indeed become a twister, spiraling to the ground.

It was recommended by this board that the flap be redesigned to incorporate a higher stressed torque tube and the inherent characteristic of the flap to retract when the torque failed to be eliminated.

The opinion of the Accident Investigating Board stated that this accident was caused by material failure. A further recommendation advised that all B-45s be grounded until all torque tubes and bearings could be replaced.

★

AMERICA ENTERS THE JET AGE

"Every time I go back to the Air Force Flight Test Center at Edwards Air Force Base, I drive slowly through the streets and gaze on the names gracing the street signs.

I knew them as men who met the challenges of new propulsion systems, new technology and new design concepts.

They paid the ultimate price as they strove to refine and solve the unknown problems that always lurk in newly developed aircraft.

They viewed their work as grim, yet fun and necessary in order that the operational pilots might have the best equipment and fewest problems."

—Brigadier General Robert (Bob) L. Cardenas, USAF (Ret.) and Chief Air Force Test Pilot for the XB-45.

In 1941, work on jet-powered aircraft was well advanced in Britain, and similar projects were underway in both Germany and Italy. However, the United States was clearly behind the rest of the world when it came to this revolutionary new form of aircraft propulsion.

In April of this same year, Major General Henry Harold "Hap" Arnold had the chance to see Britain's top-secret Gloster E-28/39 jet-powered aircraft. This new plane was powered by a W2B centrifugal turbojet designed by Wing Commander Frank Whittle, a Royal Canadian Air Force officer. The technology so impressed the General that he requested access to the craft's blueprints so America could manufacture the plane under license in the USA. Of course, the United States had been so generous with aid to Britain that his request was readily granted.

General Arnold immediately approached the General Electric Corporation of Schenectady, New York, to act as the prime American contractor for licensed production of the British jet engine. GE was known for its extensive experience with turbines for various industrial and aviation applications. Fifteen jet engines were ordered, and the production was carried out under absolute secrecy.

Bell Aircraft, also in New York, was chosen to manufacture the aircraft that would soon be powered by the new General Electric jet engines.

In the late summer of 1942, America's first jet-propelled airplane, Bell's XP-59 Airacomet, arrived at Muroc Army Air Force Base, cloaked in canvas, and concealed with a phony propeller. "Muroc" was the reversed name of the Corum family, pioneers of the Mojave Desert. They had settled on the edge of a dry lake, Rogers Dry Lake, in the late 19th century, where they established a stagecoach station for weary travelers. Muroc's very isolation and massive size made it a natural choice as a gunnery range for aircraft testing and flight training. This remote location proved well-situated, as they needed a test site that was hidden from inquisitive eyes.

The USAAF had planned to order 100 P-59A Airacomets, but its performance proved to be less than stalwart. It was rather unlikely that improvements would ever meet our military's expectations, and by the fall of 1943, the craft was no longer considered worthy. The plane never made it to operational status. The P-59A order was halved on October 30, 1943, and the Airacomet was relegated to an operational training role.

Although the Airacomet never saw service in its originally intended role as a fighter aircraft, it nevertheless provided the USAAF with valuable orientation experience in the use of jet aircraft and furnished a nucleus of trained jet pilots.

This was such a hush-hush project that hundreds of flights were made before it was revealed to the public. Once it was revealed, Muroc's mission became indelibly associated with aeronautical research, testing, and development.

The Jet-propelled Douglas XB-43.

As Muroc's facilities expanded, they eventually rivaled those found anywhere, and their work on this and other projects was carried out under maximum privacy throughout the war. Hence, the arrival of trucks bearing strangely covered cargoes did not arouse even the slightest wrinkle of anticipation outside of the individuals intimately connected to the project. Even today, this remote location is still our Nation's number one place for future military aircraft testing.

In late 1943, the USAAF initiated the "Jet Master Project," which approved two jet-propelled prototypes to be produced by the following spring. The Douglas XB-43 and the Douglas YB-43 jet masters were used only for testing of this new beast called the jet bomber. The XB-43 was a jet-propelled version of the XB-42, the last gasp of propeller driven aircraft. The XB-43 took its first flight on May17, 1946.

Robert Cardenas, retired Brigadier General, USAF, was one of the Army Air Corps' test pilots for these planes and eventually flew the final flight of the YB-43 when it was retired in 1953.

All planned purchases for further production of the YB-43 were dropped in favor of the North American B-45, which was to become our nation's first operational jet bomber. Cardenas became the Chief Air Force Test Pilot for the North American XB-45.

According to Cardenas, "When World War II ended, the United States had the most expansive air armada that man had ever seen: B-17s, B-24s, B-26s, A-26s, P-51s, and P-38s."

It's hard to believe that in 1911, the U.S. Armed Forces had only two planes and two pilots, one of them being Hap Arnold. At its peak in WWII, these numbers had grown to 2,372,292 personnel and 78,757 aircraft.

Unfortunately, this expansive air armada did not include any jets.

According to Cardenas, three factors accelerated the United States Army Air Forces' (USAAF) need to successfully design and develop America's first "operational" jet bomber.

1. We needed a plane that could break the sound barrier. Our planes were disintegrating in midair as P-51 fighter pilots chased Me109s over Germany, and aeronautical engineers determined this was the result of straight-winged aircraft approaching the speed of sound.

2. The Germans had introduced a new jet-propulsion system with the debut of their Me262 jet aircraft in 1944.

3. United States Intelligence had confirmation that Hitler was going to build more Me262s and invade England.

It was evident that the days of propeller-driven fighter planes were numbered as U.S. Intelligence received word that Hitler was planning to build an army of Me262s, which could fly circles around any USAAF aircraft. Decisive action was needed to combat the Luftwaffe's (German Air Force) eminent menace.

Fortunately, Hitler's decision to employ the Luftwaffe's jet planes as bombers rather than fighters gave the Allied bombing raids some breathing room.

J. H. "Dutch" Kindelberger, president of North American Aviation, believed that NAA could build a straightforward jet aircraft with minimal design time. While he was confident the war might be over before the aircraft could be completed, he was determined to get his plane built and off the ground.

As it turned out, Assistant Secretary Warren Lubbock met with Winston Churchill, General Dwight Eisenhower, and high military officers to discuss what the United States would do if Hitler did in fact invade England with the Luftwaffe's jet bombers. If Hitler succeeded, the Allies would no longer be able to launch attacks from their current air bases. We needed bombers and fighters that could fly greater distances in case we were forced to attack from America.

On the same night of this meeting, November 6, 1944, the Army Air Forces set into motion a project to develop aircraft that could go 10,000 miles and carry 10,000 pounds of bombs. They issued a design competition for a jet-powered bomber.

Four manufacturers submitted proposals: Convair proposed the XB-46; Martin came up with their model 233 (XB-48); North American had its NA 130 (XB-45); and Boeing with its model 424 (later to become the

B-47). Three got the nod to go ahead for production of their prototypes: North American to produce three, Martin two, and Convair, one. Ironically, Boeing had to wait until July 10, 1947, to get a contract for two prototypes of the XB-47 Stratojet. In the end, their design proved itself as the jet bomber that surpassed all others.

While these manufacturers' design teams worked feverishly to meet deadlines, WWII came to a close. Nonetheless, intense work and tight timelines continued the launch of our country's first jet bomber. Air superiority was critical for our continued fight for freedom, and jets were needed to get us there.

On May 2, 1946, the Army Air Forces assigned serial numbers to three NA-130 prototypes ordered. The ensuing XB-45 was a four jet engine airplane made by North American Aviation in Southern California. The North American B-45 was America's first operational jet bomber to employ jet propulsion and the first four-engine jet aircraft to fly in the United States. It was designed for a crew of four, consisting of the pilot, co-pilot/radio operator, bombardier-navigator, and tail gunner.

In early 1947, the first prototype was completed, dismantled, and trucked from North American's Inglewood plant on the south side of Los Angeles Municipal Airport to preserve the secrecy surrounding its development. The convoy's eventual destination was Muroc, once again the perfect location for the secret testing of jet propulsion.

Before the first of the prototypes had even flown and because of North American's sterling reputation, a contract for ninety-seven production B-45As was approved on January 20, 1947. The first reassembled prototype made its initial flight on St. Patrick's Day, March 17, 1947, with North American's test pilots, George Krebs and Paul Brewer, strapped in tandem under the bubble canopy. Because the aircraft's landing gear doors did not close properly, the one-hour flight was conducted under stringent speed

The first XB-45, 7001.
—*Jack Barham Collection, Noel Memorial Library Archives, Louisiana State University in Shreveport*

restrictions. The infringement could have been avoided by installing new and available landing gear uplocks, but they were deleted in order to not further impede the first test flight.

Nevertheless, the XB-45's fledgling ascent was impressive. No large, multi-engine jet bomber had ever flown before. An extensive test program for the three experimental prototypes then evolved, with each machine instrumented for a specialized phase of the program. If this first flight was any indication, both North American and the Army Air Forces were looking at a winner. But, no one expects a brand new airplane to be free of bugs.

Once the landing gear locks were eventually replaced, the second flight occurred on March 26 for two hours and fourteen minutes in the air.

XB-45 Phase Two test team: Schmidt, Cardenas, Edwards & Forbes. Wright Field, Dayton, OH.

The XB-45 subsequently settled down to a continuous program of testing and modifications. The first Air Force pilots to fly the XB-45 were Major Robert Cardenas and Captain Glen Edwards. In addition, Daniel Forbes served as co-pilot on these test flights. Muroc was later renamed Edwards Air Force Base, in honor of Edwards who perished along with Forbes in the crash of one of the only two Northrop YB-49 Flying Wings ever produced.

However, if anyone thought the plane was a home run with nothing more than a quick fix of the gear door latches, they were wrong.

As further testing progressed, two major problems appeared. Entry and exit from the XB-45's cockpit and bombardier's station were through a door in the fuselage nose, as the bubble canopy was fixed to maintain pressurization. In the event of an emergency, crewmembers would have to unstrap, work their way through the access passageway from the flight deck, and leap out through the side door. The navigator-bombardier would also exit through this same door while the tail gunner popped an emergency hatch in the right side and rolled out to safety.

Unfortunately, it was highly possible that this extended escape route could cause the loss of one or both of the men. Further testing did little to pacify this fear. An alternative method to exit would have the pilot and co-pilot open the bomb bay doors, crawl through an access hatch at the rear cockpit bulkhead, and jump through the wide-open hole in the plane's belly. It looked fine in theory; however, the slipstream caught and hurled the first test dummy from the forward bomb bay against the rear bulkhead of the bomb bay. There was reason to believe that a man would receive the same treatment. The slipstream also made opening the access door in flight a treacherous operation, although once clear of it, a bailout became as normal as could be expected.

North American's engineers returned to their drafting tables to eliminate this hazard as rapidly as possible. The dummy's spectacular demise resulted in an immediate redesign of the initial batch of production aircraft and a quick retrofit for the prototypes. Spring-loaded flaps installed ahead of both the door and the escape hatch for the tail gunner would counter the buffeting caused by the slipstream.

When design work on the B-45 began, ejection seats had barely reached the experimental stage in this country. A step ahead of the U.S., the Luftwaffe's Heinkel He219A Uhu ("Owl") night fighter was equipped with seats propelled by compressed air. England's Martin-Baker Company had also developed a system using an exploding powder charge to propel the pilot's seat vertically along rails anchored to the rear cockpit protective armor plate.

A second, more serious problem affected the flight controls. The original design had the port and starboard controls working off separate hydraulic systems, with conventional mechanical backups. However, since these mirror-image systems were independent of each other, even in the event of a partial failure, only one side would revert to mechanical operation. This would create a chaotic situation in which the pilot and co-pilot would be hard pressed to control the airplane. To correct this possibility, the B-45's hydraulic systems were linked together through cross-connections. In the event of a failure, the controls reverted to manual power.

As events proved, the B-45 was prone to hydraulic blowouts. This malfunction often occurred during takeoff, which caused the plane to exhibit a spine-tingling inclination to roll before the pilot and co-pilot could bring it under control. Many accidents were attributed to this engineering oversight.

According to Cardenas, another challenge became evident with the B-45s during jet-assisted-take-offs (JATO). Two jet rockets with 4,000 pounds of thrust and 60-second durations, were mounted under each nacelle. There was no throttle to adjust the jet rockets, just an on/off switch.

Cardenas recalled one of his many eventful flights in the B-45 when only one of his jets fired. In later jet bombers this problem was corrected by placing the jet rockets in the tail so they would be in line with the flight of the aircraft.

Landing without brakes was justifiably challenging. It was fortunate that military airfields are built with long runways. Even then, many B-45s wound up off the end of the pavement. Braking parachutes were another luxury that the plane's designers had neglected to provide.

B-45 during jet-assisted-take-off (JATO).

Following the conclusion of its initial test program, the XB-45 prototype underwent additional flight and systems evaluation. Cardenas, Edwards, Forbes, and Engineer, Richard Schmidt took on Phase Two testing of the XB-45. At the same time, this team was responsible to test Convair's single prototype of the XB-46. They continually swapped airplanes to determine the better of the two planes. One day, Cardenas, with Forbes as co-pilot, would fly the XB-45, and the next day, Edwards, with Forbes as co-pilot, would fly the XB-46.

As Cardenas now recalls, "As chief Army Air Corps' test pilots, each of us received a kneepad with a clip for notecards, a #2H pencil, and a stopwatch."

"Although," he smiles, "some of us did have a slide rule!"

Convair's XB-46 flown by test pilots Cardenas & Edwards. Photo signed by Edwards.

Testing between the XB-45 and XB-46 continued until the decision was made to drop the latter because of, as Cardenas recalls it, "The twang that occurred when the XB-46 was in turbulence."

Its long nose turned out to be a bit too long.

The first XB-45 prototype then returned to Long Beach, California, during the summer of 1948 to be outfitted with General Electric's new TG-190, a turbojet engine rated at 5,200 pounds static thrust. It was subsequently designated as the J47, one of the most widely produced jet engines in aviation history. This conversion may very well have been a contributing factor to the tragic events of September 20, 1948.

On that day, Krebs, who had been one of the test pilots for the early flights, took the number one XB-45 prototype up for routine stability and cooling tests with another North American company pilot, Nick Piccard. This was the sixty-ninth flight and the last one for plane number 45-59479 and for aviation pioneers Krebs and Piccard. Thus far, it had been a near-flawless test platform. This XB-45's fatal crash inevitably resulted in a lengthy inquiry into its cause and ways to prevent it from happening again.

The remaining two XB-45 prototypes took on the entire flight-test load, although Air Force pilots did not participate extensively in the initial tests. They flew only about 19 hours, while the contractor logged more than 165 flight hours on the two surviving aircraft. A total of 131 flights were conducted before the Air Force took delivery of the planes. North American and the Air Force continued to investigate the capabilities and limitations even as production aircraft came off the line at Long Beach.

Due to one of the frequent postwar budget battles and cutbacks in defense appropriations, in 1948, the newly autonomous U.S. Air Force accepted the necessity of ferrying the new B-45s directly from the Long Beach factory to Norton Air Force Base on the outskirts of San Bernardino, California. Cocooned in storage there, the planes awaited the necessary operational funds. As it turned out, this base came to know the B-45s well. Norton was designated as the prime support center for depot-level maintenance throughout its service career.

The initial Air Force group to receive the B-45s was the 47th Bomb Group of the Twelfth Air Force, located at Biggs Air Force Base in El Paso, Texas. Major Cardenas flew the first B-45 into Biggs. When he flew back to Muroc, he took the wing navigator with him. It was a night flight, and the navigator was in awe at the speed in which the lights passed beneath them. He was not accustomed to plotting locations at speeds in excess of 500 miles per hour.

Col. Chapman briefing the press, Nov. 1948.
—Jack Barham Collection, Noel Memorial Library Archives, Louisiana State University in Shreveport

Since the B-45 needed longer runways, the 47th Bomb Group said goodbye to Biggs and was relocated to Barksdale Air Force Base in Shreveport, Louisiana. On February 24, 1948, Colonel Willis F. Chapman, Commanding Officer of the group, flew the first of the B-45As from California to Louisiana, with a stopover at the 47th Bomb Group's old home, Biggs Air Force Base in Texas. Chapman's maiden flight was seven months before the prototype XB-45 crash at Muroc that proved fatal for test pilots, Krebs and Piccard.

The new aircraft were eventually released from storage and flown from Norton to Barksdale Air Force Base, Louisiana, where they joined the

Col. Chapman explains the B-45s flight range.
—Jack Barham Collection, Noel Memorial Library Archives, Louisiana State University in Shreveport

84th and 85th Bombardment Squadrons. They were a welcome replacement to the aging prop-driven B-26 Invaders. Unit price for the B-45A was a mere $769,700.

The B-45A differed from the prototype in featuring improved ejection-type seats for the pilot and co-pilot and safer emergency escape hatches for the bombardier-navigator and tail gunner. Communication equipment, emergency flight controls, and instruments installed at the co-pilot's station were also new. Other improvements included the E-4 automatic pilot, a bombing-navigation radar, and A-1 fire-control system; all of which were standard equipment.

The 47th Bomb Group welcomes the B-45, their new plane and the nation's first jet bomber.
—*Jack Barham Collection, Noel Memorial Library Archives, Louisiana State University in Shreveport*

Three squadrons learned the basics with six weeks of ground training on a Mobile Training Unit (MTU). A detachment of twenty-two officers and eighty-four senior enlisted men traveled west to Edwards Air Force Base (formerly Muroc) for an intensive conversion-training course under the direction of Cardenas. At the completion of this, the group considered itself operational and ready to begin work.

The 47th Bomb Group's conversion to the B-45s was not without excitement. On three occasions, the enclosure over the navigator-bombardier's station in the nose blew out at high altitudes. Fortunately, it was standard procedure to wear an oxygen mask at all times, so while these structural failures were startling, they caused no major injuries. North American corrected this deficiency by adding stiffening bracing to the cockpit canopy, strengthening of the greenhouse over the bombardier-navigator's position, and retrofitting those structures on planes as they returned to Norton Air Force Base for servicing.

It is a mystery today if the blowout tendency on one of the first three B-45 planes sent to the 47th Bomb Group was to play a major factor in saving the life of James L. Louden, Captain, United States Air Force. Had he not been blown from the plane, he may not have lived to tell his story.

Coupled with the frequent hydraulic system failures, such mishaps undoubtedly kept life in the 47th far from routine and dull. It is no wonder that the 47th Bomb Group voted to name it the B-45 Tornado!

By 1949, when the B-45C version appeared, the Air Force decided it needed a long-range photoreconnaissance machine to replace the veteran Boeing RB-29A Superfort. North American received instructions to investigate methods for modifying the Tornado to carry a variety of aerial cameras.

The contract for the B-45C, AC18000, approved November 13, 1947, was modified to cover production of thirty-three photoreconnaissance NA-153 RB-45Cs.

The first of the RB-45s flew at Long Beach, California, in December 1949, with deliveries to Air Force squadrons beginning in June 1950.

Air Force 48-011 (RB-45) carried a crew of three on its maiden flight, including Air Force Majors T. B. McGuire, C. H. Barnett, and Captain Charles (Chuck) F. Yeager. Yeager had previously gained notoriety on October 14, 1947, when he flew the Bell XS-1 rocket plane past the speed of sound and lived to tell about it.

Signed photo by Chuck Yeager taken from the cockpit of the RB-45 at 50,000 feet.

The event marked a new era in aviation history. Yeager knew the risks, as prior attempts by the British had proven fatal. He climbed into the XS-I, which lay waiting in the belly of the airborne B-29, flown by Cardenas and his co-pilot Capt. Jackie Ridley. At 20,000 feet, Yeager dropped out of the B-29 with all four rockets firing. Following behind were two chase planes. Within seconds, the team heard the world's first sonic boom as the XS-I reached Mach 1.06 (700 miles per hour).

Yeager went on to become one of the world's most famous test pilots and retired as a Brigadier General.

XS-1 and its team on October 14, 1947, the day they made history.

The Team That Broke The Sound Barrier

Back row left to right:

Lt. Bob Hoover– alternate XS-1 pilot and chase pilot

Maj. Dick Frost– from Bell Aircraft and second chase pilot

Front row left to right:

Lt. Ed Swindell– flight engineer

Major Bob Cardenas– project officer in charge and B-29 launch pilot

Capt. Chuck Yeager–XS-1 pilot

Capt. Jackie Ridley– project test engineer and B-29 co-pilot

In 1950, the 47th Bomb Group, still under the command of General Chapman, moved from Barksdale to Langley Air Force Base in Norfolk, Virginia. This proved to be its last U.S. home. In the fall of 1952, The 47th Bomb Group arrived in RAF Station Sculthorpe, just North East of London. According to retired Col. Eric Linhof, USAF, the 84th Bomb Squadrons later joined the 47th.

While in England, they were assigned to tactical air command, with their focus on targeting Soviet Union airfields in Easter Europe. Thirty thousand missions later, the B-45 retired in 1958 and was replaced by the Douglas B-66. Most B-45s were dismantled and used for parts. We found two B-45s currently on display in the United States today. An RB-45C is in the USAF Museum at Wright Patterson Air Force Base in Dayton, Ohio. The second, the B-45A, is located at the Castle Air Museum, near Castle Air Force Base in Atwater, California.

It's truly amazing how far we have come with aviation technology since the Wright brothers and the first planes that flew in WWI. We can only imagine what technology advances lay ahead for both air and space travel. Experts predict that the next major breakthrough in flight will be unmanned, computer-driven aircraft that promise amazing accuracy in reconnaissance and combat missions without the need to risk lives.

For this incredible aeronautical technology to take flight, there will continue to be exceptional men and women who hold the key by turning visions into realities. Thanks to all those aviation pioneers with their special talents, adventuresome spirits and can-do attitudes. God bless those who have come before and all those who will continue to advance the wonders of flight.

ON GOD'S WINGS

Brigadier General Robert L. Cardenas (Ret.)

Bob Cardenas as a young test pilot, stepping out of the B-45 Tornado.

Brigadier General Cardenas (Ret.) is one of America's few living aviation legends. It is because of men like Cardenas that America has made gigantic steps in the race to superior flight. As a test pilot for the United States Air Force, he helped forge our nation's air armada and has been witness to major milestones including the testing of America's first operational jet bomber – the B-45 Tornado.

Cardenas has flown more than 60 different aircraft in his career, including the flight test evaluation of the German jet fighter ME-262 and the Arado 234 bomber. In 1947 he served as the project officer and command pilot of the B-29 that launched Captain Charles Yeager into supersonic flight.

After his service in the Korean War, Cardenas returned to Washington D.C. where he was assigned to the Pentagon as Chief of the Aircraft and Missiles Program Division. From there he was assigned Chief of the Special Operations Division at US Strike Command Headquarters in Tampa, Florida. In 1962 he led a joint Army & Air Force Special Force into Kashmir, India where he evaluated and improved high altitude re-supply drops in the Himalayan Mountains. He used these techniques to equip forces and prevented an incursion of Chinese through the Himalayas linking into East Pakistan.

In 1968 Cardenas was promoted to Brigadier General and he was placed in command of the Air Force Special Operations Force at Eglin and Hurlburt AFB, Florida.

Cardenas has been honored with the Distinguished Service Medal, Legion of Merit with Oak Leaf Cluster, Distinguished Flying Cross, Purple Heart, Meritorious Service Medal, Air Medal with Four Oak Leaf Clusters, Joint Service Commendation Medal, Air Force Commendation Medal with Oak Leaf Cluster and the Presidential Citation. His foreign decorations include the Spanish Grand Legion of Aeronautical Merit with Shash and Dagger.

The USAF Test Pilot School at Edwards AFB honored the General in 1994 as a Distinguished Alumnus and in 1995 he was inducted into the Aerospace Walk of Honor at Lancaster, California. In 2002, Cardenas was inducted into the Air Commando Hall of Fame.

Living legends, Jim & Cardenas share incredible memories of the B-45 Tornado, 2004.

His list of many medals, honors and accolades goes on, as does his legend. Although the Brigadier General retired from the Air Force in 1973, he has continued to serve his country with pride in a variety of capacities. He currently serves as a member of the San Diego Mayor's Veteran Advisory Board, Chairman of the Veteran's Memorial Museum and Center, as well as a Trustee of the Flight Test Historical Foundation at Edwards AFB.

BIG JIM'S POST-CRASH MILITARY CAREER

"It's not whether you get knocked down.
It's whether you get up again."

— Vince Lombardi

Jim's best friend, Leo Paul Roberts, far left/back row, pilot of B-26 Marauder,
May 1944. —Rhonda Roberts Glasscock collection

Jim Louden and Leo Paul Roberts had established a deep kinship during World War II when they flew B-26 Marauder missions together. This friendship strengthened while they were both stationed at air bases in Texas and Louisiana. Dad nicknamed his good friend Leepe, and they shared many fun times together. Their wives, Peggy and Pat, also became close as they followed their husbands from state to state, base to base.

BIG JIM'S POST-CRASH MILITARY CAREER

"It was a country club life in those post war days," Pat Roberts (now Pat Coleman) says with her smooth Southern accent from her early years in Memphis, Tennessee. "We were one big extended family. Bridge games by the club pool and great parties at the Officers' Club, where we danced to Big Band sounds and of course Jim's often requested *Peg O' My Heart*."

Peg O' My Heart

Peg O' my heart, I love you
Don't let us part, I love you
I always knew, it would be you,
Since I heard your lilting laughter
It's your Irish heart I'm after
Peg O' my heart, your glances
Make my heart say, how's Chances
Come be my own, come make your home
In my heart

Peg O' my heart, I love you
We'll never part, I love you
Dear little girl, sweet little girl
Sweeter than the Rose of Erin
Are your winning smiles endearing

Peg O' my heart, your glances
With Irish art, entrance us
Come be my own, come make your home
In my heart

Fun at Barksdale Officers' Club, Feb. 19, 1949.

"The guys flew together, golfed together, and partied together, just like a fraternity. And of course 'Big Jim' was always the life of the party with his harmonica medleys."

"None of them ever thought what they did was work. Are you kidding? They were doing what they loved, flyin' airplanes."

"Most of them had flown combat in World War II, and from that experience, they developed a deep and common bond. They had successfully defended America's freedoms and democracy."

"We wives, in those days, shared the same spirit of love for the American dream. We knew that our role was to support our husbands and the military."

"And we did support them, no matter what it took, which often meant moving. And moving. And moving again. Good grief, we became really good at moving!"

"The 47th Bomb Group was a good example. First our group was stationed in Biggs Field in El Paso, Texas. Six-hundred men and their families. And then the Air Force tells us to move, lock, stock and barrel, to Barksdale in Shreveport, Louisiana. Why? Because the runway for the new B-45 Tornado jet bomber needed to be longer than the 5,000-foot runway at Biggs Field. At Barksdale, the runway was 10,000 feet. Then, in early 1950, they moved us again... this time to Langley Air Force Base in Norfolk, Virginia."

"But, you know, we adopted the spirit, especially the wives of the 47th Bomb Group, that we were 'in it together.' What an amazing spirit and support group we developed!"

When news of Jim's crash reached Leo and Pat, on leave at the time, they rushed back to look after Peggy, helping her through her shock and to cope with stress and uncertainty. When Jim regained consciousness, the Roberts were there to encourage him on his rough road of recovery and to provide emotional support for Peggy.

The Tables Turn

A year after the crash, while Jim was undergoing physical therapy at Walter Reed, his 47th Bomb Group had once again been transferred, this time to Langley Air Force Base in Hampton, Virginia. And as the miracle of Jim's recovery unfolded, a second miracle had presented itself to this young couple in the form of their firstborn. Young James Leslie Louden, Jr., or J.L., as my older brother was called in his early years, was born at Walter Reed Army Medical Center on August 28, 1950. Being from Pittsburgh, home of J&L Steel, his nickname, J.L., had special meaning to our family.

Now as Peggy would continue to spend most of her days at Walter Reed, spurring Jim onward in his rehabilitation efforts, she was also holding their firstborn: new life, new hope, a new day...

Jim had survived. They had overcome adversity. Life was good; there was so much hope.

And then Peggy received a telephone call from Col. Chapman of the 47th Bomb Group. The number-one engine in a B-45 had blown in midair at 40,000 feet. The explosion blew off a wing, and the plane plummeted straight down. The entire crew had been lost.

Leo Roberts was one of them.

Peggy heard the words, but comprehension was slow to come. She heard the words, and she even was able to relay them to Jim. But she was numb.

Was Jim well enough to travel down to Virginia to be an honorary pallbearer at Leo's funeral?

Funeral? Another B-45 crash?... I can only imagine my mother's mind trying to keep up with the news that Col. Chapman was communicating. Explosion. Wing blown off. Leo... dead. Oh my God... Pat! Pat and her two toddlers.

For Jim, having to face the loss of his best friend was intensely painful, but to know it was at the hands of a B-45 was agonizing.

This had come so close to being Jim's fate. The Roberts had just months before been the ones comforting Peggy, and championing Jim as he progressed in his recovery. They had been wonderful.

And now, Jim and Peggy Louden were the ones who would need to be the stalwarts for Pat.

Peggy drove Jim to Hampton, Virginia, to attend the funeral. The ride down was eerily quiet. Yes, they would find the strength to comfort Pat. They steeled themselves; Jim against the pain writhing through his body, as he positioned himself for an agonizing but necessary ride; Peggy against the pain of grief for her dear friend and the fear of what would lay ahead for her own husband.

They attended the service, full of military tradition, compassion, and respect. The American flag that had covered Leo's coffin was ceremoniously and meticulously folded 13 times, with each fold carrying with it symbolism:

The first fold is a symbol of life;

The second fold is a symbol of our belief in eternal life;

The third fold is made in honor and remembrance of the veterans departing our ranks who gave a portion of their lives for the defense of our country to attain peace throughout the world;

The fourth fold represents our weaker nature, for as American citizens trusting in God, it is to Him we turn in times of peace as well as in time of war for His divine guidance;

The fifth fold is a tribute to our country, for in the words of Stephen Decatur, "Our country, in dealing with other countries, may she always be right, but it is still our country, right or wrong;"

The sixth fold is for where our hearts lie. It is with our heart that we pledge allegiance to the flag of the United States of America and to the Republic for which it stands, one nation under God, indivisible, with liberty and justice for all;

The seventh fold is a tribute to our armed forces, for it is through the armed forces that we protect our country and our flag against all her enemies, whether they be found within or without the boundaries of our republic;

The eighth fold is a tribute to the one who entered the valley of the shadow of death, that we might see the light of day and to honor mother, for whom it flies on Mother's Day;

The ninth fold is a tribute to womanhood, for it has been through their faith, their loyalty and devotion that the character of the men and women who have made our country great has been molded;

The tenth fold is a tribute to father, for he, too, has given his sons and daughters for the defense of our country since they were first born;

The eleventh fold, in the eyes of a Hebrew citizen, represents the lower portion of the seal of King David and King Solomon and glorifies in their eyes the God of Abraham, Isaac, and Jacob;

The twelfth fold, in the eyes of a Christian citizen, represents an emblem of eternity and glorifies in their eyes, God the Father, the Son, and the Holy Spirit;

The thirteenth fold, when the flag is completely folded, the stars are uppermost, reminding us of our nation's motto, "In God we trust."

And then from the outstretched and gloved hands of a military officer, expressing the thanks of a grateful nation, Pat Roberts received the flag of our nation.

Dad relied on his Christian scripture to guide Pat on life's journey. Mom reached out to hold and comfort her friend, day and night. They spoke with Pat's parents, played with her children, let her see their new arrival, little J.L. They promised to get together soon.

And then it was over. My parents drove back to Walter Reed; Dad in severe pain after several days of car travel and a show of mental and physical strength he barely had been able to muster. My mother in a silent pain of grief for her friend and apprehension of what would lay around the next corner, beyond the next cloud, in her life with my dad.

And as my parents headed back to the long road of rehabilitation, Pat faced the need for a new way of life. She was told she must relinquish her base housing in short order. And, with only a minimal life-insurance payment for military wives in those days, she had to think of how she would provide for herself and two children, Rhonda, just 3 months old, and Ben, nearly 3 years old. Like most of the young military widows who came before her, Pat relied on her parents to pull her through her grief and to provide a safe harbor. She and her children returned home to live with them briefly as she gathered strength and a new life plan. Pat was a talented and social young woman, and she needed every ounce of her tenacity to rise to life's new challenges. She returned to her career as an airline stewardess. Yes, "stewardess" was the 1950s description of today's "flight attendant," and the performance criteria of the era included: attractive female, well-coiffed hair, exquisitely applied makeup, ideal weight, and poise. Delta Airlines had to "bend the rules" to hire Pat; in those days stewardesses could not be, nor have ever been, married; nor could they have children. Pat hired a nanny to assist with childcare, worked for Delta for 10 years, and eventually remarried.

Up, Up, and Away!

Jim Louden was offered permanent physical disability compensation to finish his career on active duty by the Air Force; to Peggy's chagrin, he turned it down.

He not only wanted to return to active duty but also to return to flying airplanes. Despite the crash, he still loved to fly, loved to serve his country, and, now more than ever, believed in following whatever path was revealed to him in his prayers.

I can only imagine that my mother was devastated by his decision. But, by this time, she knew that anything she said was useless. Her husband had almost died, and he had just seen his best friend buried after his plane had crashed high-in-the-skies. If those circumstances didn't deter Jim from his conquest of the skies, she knew nothing she said would have any effect. She accepted his fate as hers. She kept quiet to maintain a happy marriage. And yet, how frustrated she must have been.

Col. Chapman recognized Jim's determination to continue his career and supported his commitment by obtaining approval from the Pentagon, requesting that, upon his release from Walter Reed, Louden be allowed to rejoin the 47th as the group's public information officer.

He then had to pass physical, mental, and psychological tests to be accepted once more into the military "flying club," including the potential for flying in war.

He passed the tests, and on April Fools' Day, 1951, Jim rejoined his unit at Langley Air Force Base in Norfolk, Virginia. He had fooled them all by surviving and coming back to fly again, this time in DC-3s and A-26s.

That September, Dad was promoted to Major.

A year later, as the Korean "Police Action" heated up into war, Jim was transferred to Nagoya, Japan, where he continuously flew troops, equipment, and supplies into Korea, returning with wounded Army soldiers who would receive care at the base hospital. It was at this very hospital in Nagoya where I came into the world on July 2, 1953.

Back in the USA

From Japan, we headed to March Air Force Base in Riverside, California. At this Strategic Air Command (SAC) base, dad flew KC-97s, a Boeing air-refueling plane that refueled bombers and fighters while in the air. Introduced in 1950, this plane used the flying boom refueling system; eventually KC-135 jet tankers replaced this plane. Dad also ran the KC-97 simulator, which was used to train future crews.

In keeping with our military life, our time in sunny Southern California lasted but a few years and it was time to move on. This time, we were off to experience the Midwest. While his duties and flying of the KC-97 remained the same, we were now in Columbus, Ohio, at another SAC base, Lockborne Air Force Base, now Rickbenbaker AFB. With the cold war getting hotter, Dad was called for new training and given a new assignment. It was once again time to move on. He attended the missile training school in Huntsville, Alabama, where he learned how to operate and launch the Chrysler-made Jupiter Guided Missiles. There were 15 of these missiles located in Izmir, Turkey, aimed at southern Soviet Union. And, in like fashion, the Soviet Union had their missiles aimed at us.

The Cuban Missile Crisis

In February of 1962, Jim reported to his next assignment in Izmir, Turkey at Cigli Air Base. There he served as Launch Site Commander, then Deputy Commander. A major focus of the group was to teach the Turkish military personnel how to operate and launch these missiles.

In keeping with Dad's love of flying, he was grateful that his duties also included delivering supplies and personnel to South East Europe and the Mediterranean in the Air Force's C-47. This jet air-transport plane is also known as the DC-3, the Sky Train, and the Gooney Bird. I remember he particularly enjoyed his unique opportunity to see many of the beautiful islands off the coast of Greece and Turkey, including Crete and Cyprus.

In March of 1962, while in Turkey, Dad received his promotion to Lieutenant Colonel, a rank he proudly held upon retirement.

This Cold War was a different type of war than my dad, or anyone for that matter, had ever experienced. In October 1962, at the height of the Cuban Missile Crisis, a message arrived from the War Department in Washington, D.C. It ordered the base to get the missiles off target immediately.

It was baffling. Communication was slow and intermittent in this era that pre-dated satellite communication and the Internet. There was no television in Turkey, and even *The Stars and Stripes* newspaper often arrived days late. No one on the base could comprehend the moment-by-moment crisis decision dealings between President John F. Kennedy and Soviet Premier Khrushchev. But Dad and his fellow officers did understand that an order was an order. The agreement arrived just in the nick of time between these two world powers to avert World War III. The Soviet Union would take their missiles out of Cuba if America would take 15 missiles out of Turkey and 30 missiles out of Italy.

Possible World War III averted, Christmas of 1963 had a wonderful treat in store for Cigli Air Force Base. Bob Hope with his entire USO Troop arrived to perform. His entourage included Les Brown and his Band of Renown; Miss America, Anita Bryant; Tuesday Weld; and popular comedian, Jerry Colonna. Lt. Col. Louden, as Deputy Base Commander, met their plane, greeted everyone, and remembers escorting Les Brown to the Visiting Officers' Quarters. I can remember sitting through the whole show – and, yes, Bob Hope was as incredible as ever. Thanks for the memory, Bob!

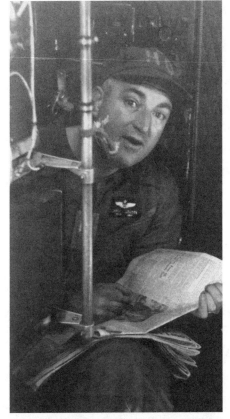

An in-flight newsbreak, Jan. 1959.

Big Jim's Post-Crash Military Career

Minute Man Missiles

In July of 1964, we all returned to the United States. Dad was stationed at Francis E. Warren Air Force Base in Cheyenne, Wyoming for the next year and a half where he was Deputy Commander of the Minute Man Missile Squadron. This squadron was responsible for 50 Long Range Intercontinental Minute Man One Missiles housed in underground silos in three states – Wyoming, South Dakota, and Kansas. Dad would check the morale of the men stationed at each underground base. These men were in the Strategic Air Command and charged with the top-secret codes that could launch these missiles to hit any target in the world.

Vietnam and the Last Assignment

The Cold War crisis was abated, but Vietnam was intensifying, and the Air Force was short on pilots. Early in 1966, "Big Jim" was called back to the cockpit and took a six-week training course at Sewart Air Force Base in Smyrna, Tennessee. This time, he would learn to fly the C-130, a four-engine transport airplane made by Lockheed. This was to be the last plane of his career.

Once again, Dad found a plane he would love and was called to fly in the Dominican Republic uprising. For the next several months, he flew C-130 missions to the Dominican Republic where rebels were attempting to overthrow the government. America came to the aid of the regime. Dad's C-130 missions delivered fresh troops and supplies from Pope Air Force Base in Fayetteville, North Carolina, and returned with the wounded and injured soldiers.

Yes, our family moved once again, this time leaving the wild open spaces of Cheyenne for Fayetteville, North Carolina. It was time for us to experience yet another region of the country, the South. Dad had preceded us to take his pre-flight training in the C-130; he then returned to gather up our family.

Mom, with our able-bodied assistance, had, once again, packed up one house and was ready to greet a new home across the country. This time, Dad drove one car, and Mom followed behind.

"Big Jim" would spend the last five years of his military career at Pope Air Force Base, and Fayetteville was to be Peggy's last move. Home at last!

North to Alaska

Not to say Dad wasn't still on the go. The following summer, Lt. Col. Louden was moved from the tropics to the tundra, when he became Base Commander at King Salmon Air Force Base in Alaska. At the base's 10,000-foot runway strip, two F102 fighters and two F106 fighters, all with nuclear weapons under their wings, were poised for immediate action, 24 hours a day, 365 days a year. The Cold War waged on, and King Salmon was the closest base at striking distance to the Soviet Union.

Dad may have been without family for this stint of service, but he wasn't without visitors, with the base receiving Vice President Hubert H. Humphrey and several U.S. Senators. The King and Queen of Nepal stopped by, and extended an invitation for Lt. Col. Louden and his wife, Peggy, to travel to Katmandu as their guests. This is one trip they never made, but knowing Dad, he just might make it yet.

Santa Claus came calling on the Eskimo kids that December. Dad got the idea to dress up as Santa and flew in a helicopter to all the nearby Eskimo villages, armed with a bagful of toys, which he dispensed with a mighty "ho, ho, ho" from his whirring "sleigh."

But not all times were as gleeful. In January 1968, something happened that was devastating to this Base Commander. King Salmon's runway was to remain open at all times under all circumstances. After months of training, a big exercise was scheduled. And the night before, the skies let loose with snow and ice, as winds up to 60 miles per hour roared in from the Bering

Santa Jim and his air sleigh, Dec. 1967.

Sea. The temperature plunged below freezing. Dad and the civil engineers under him moved heaven and earth to prevent ice from forming and cleared snow off the runway all night long in preparation for an 8 a.m. landing of the squadron of planes from Anchorage.

Conditions made it impossible. As Commander, Dad was responsible, and because of this incident, he was relieved of his command at King Salmon. He was transferred to Shemya Air Force Base on the last island of the Aleutian Islands. He became the Base Operations Officer and spent his last five months of his command there.

This was an act of God that Dad had to accept. In this remote outpost, he knew he had to carry on and move forward. Considering how many wonderful acts of God he had received in his life, he knew he could handle this one setback.

Dad's tour in Alaska was a tough time for my brother and me. We were in our formative years; I was in junior high, and my brother was in high school. We missed him at sporting events, holiday celebrations, award ceremonies, and at our lively family dinner discussions, which he always made livelier. In those days, before computers and video recorders, we sent audiotapes back and forth to try and maintain ongoing communication. My mom, brother, and I had no trouble

Teri & J.L. welcome dad home from Alaska.

filling up an hour-long tape since we each could share our respective stories and latest news. However, it was painful on our end to listen to poor Dad trying to fill up his entire tape with news from his remote Alaska location. Needless to say, he filled the gap with harmonica tunes along with a few jokes.

In July 1968, Dad finally returned to Pope Air Force Base where our family was waiting. Hugs, kisses, catching up... but it wouldn't be long before we'd be waving him goodbye in the opposite direction.

The following May, Lt. Col. Louden, the accomplished pilot of the C-130, was needed for a highly classified mission in Vietnam for three months. Peggy knew better than to question his decision to volunteer. Yes, he wanted to go to Vietnam; a number of his friends had been in action there, and this was his chance. And he loved that C-130.

Lt. Col. Louden's mission turned out to be a grueling but exciting tactical reconnaissance operation to tape the Viet Cong. He flew the C-130 Baker Model, unescorted, at 30,000 feet over the nation of Laos, using radar equipment to tape the enemy. Each flight lasted 10 hours; he'd fly to DaNang, drop off a sack full of tapes, without shutting off the engines, then immediately fly back to Cam Ron Bay. He'd be briefed on weather conditions, his plane loaded with fuel, radar equipment, and tapes; one day on, one day off... ninety days straight. Mission accomplished. He returned home from his days in the intense Vietnamese sun, and I remember him having the darkest tan I had ever seen on him. Dad then finished out his career at Pope Air Force Base. This time Lt. Col. Louden was home at last.

On April 1, 1971, Lt. Col. James L. Louden retired after almost 30 years of continuous service. He had flown more than 6,000 hours – including more than 650 hours of combat time – in twenty types of aircraft, earning the Distinguished Flying Cross and fifteen other air medals.

"Big Jim" was now making plans for the next chapter of his life. "Jim, you are going to live to be 100," Mom told him, "and that's because you never worry about a damn thing!"

Chuckling, Dad said he had to agree. His career clearly demonstrated to both of them that he had "no fear." He had flown combat in four arenas, been hit and nearly downed over the English Channel by anti-aircraft fire, lived through two crashes, and sustained life-threatening injuries. But he always recovered and came back with more faith in life than ever. With his positive mental attitude, love for people, and incredible faith in Jesus Christ, "Big Jim," now 50, was just revving up for "middle age." After all, he was only at the halfway point to 100!

★

THE LOUDEN FAMILY TRAVELS

"Happiness is not a destination. It is a method of life."

— Burton Hills

I grew up with a double education: sound classroom learning integrated with exposure to international cultures.

This experience played a major role in shaping my life and the way I view the world. Perhaps this real-world education was one of the essential components that propelled me to make good grades and, in turn, earn a college scholarship. And I know that my travels throughout the world led me to become a person who appreciates the joys and wonders of cultural diversity and individual differences. It certainly made me appreciative of being a citizen of the United States. As a woman, I thank God that I live in a country where women have so many opportunities and freedoms that are not available elsewhere.

Throughout my childhood, we moved approximately once every two years, but for me, that was no problem at all. I embraced each new destination and relished soaking up history and sites. I give tribute to my mother for making each new house and city our home. She made each move not a burden, but a joyous adventure. As a result, I am a person who not only manages, but thrives on change, which I consider a gift since life is filled with constant change, and today the pace of change is ever-accelerating.

As I think back on my formative years, I realize that there was much spirituality connected with our Louden family travels. I grew up singing in the choirs at each chapel on our different base locations, and participated in Bible studies. I was fortunate that my family traveled to places like the Holy Land and Jerusalem — each trip gave a deeper meaning to my teachings.

From my birthplace in Nagoya, Japan, to travels throughout the Middle East and Europe, I became aware at a young age that one's culture strongly influences what a person considers important in life. And "success" itself becomes an amorphous term, defined quite differently from country to country, culture to culture.

To me, success includes a great deal of independence, allowing me to be in control of my destiny. I grew up believing that my future was limited only by my own creativity, and I was ready to grab every brass ring in my path.

My first introduction to living in the United States was at March Air Force Base in Riverside, California. While my mother no doubt missed her beautiful Japanese mansion, I loved our new California home where I could partake from the fruit of an orange tree in our backyard. I will never forget how wonderfully sweet those oranges were, and, of course, the endless days of sunshine in Southern California. It was the mid '50s, and I was just entering kindergarten.

I was four-years-old, and I had never lived in the U.S. My parents got me excited about this first move… we were going to California – home of the brand new Disneyland and Knott's Berry Farm, too. We'd have sandy beaches and sunshine every day. It was all true. We went to the beach, and we spent New Year's Day at the Rose Bowl Parade. I learned to ride a bike and roller-skate, and we had picnics at the redwood table in our backyard.

At Halloween, I wore my Japanese kimono and my wooden shoes with their velvet straps. The other kids all had traditional American costumes: fairy princesses, witches, ghosts, and goblins. My costume was really not a costume at all – it was authentic Japanese dress, and it was completely foreign to them. I was different, and yet, I knew it was okay. In fact, in my mind, it was more than okay; it was fun. That theme would lead me to a life of "dare to be different."

This first move began the foundation of my thoughts on change– change was a good thing. I was six-years-old in 1959, and we were transferred to Columbus, Ohio, where my dad served at Lockborne Air Force Base. To help my brother and me say goodbye to our friends in California, Mom hosted an outdoor picnic party for us, all the while contending with the movers who were packing up our household goods. All I remember is the party, thanks to my mom. It is likely that she would remember that day a bit differently!

But, our move to Columbus was short-lived. Our country was deeply entangled in the Cold War when Dad was transferred in February 1962 to a brand-new military base, Cigli, in Izmer, Turkey. A port on the Aegean Sea, it was a pretty city located on a glistening bay. Dad served as a missile launch officer for 15 Jupiter missiles housed above ground in the hilly terrain, all within 25 miles of the base. The missiles were aimed at Russia and the Cigli base was on high security.

At the time of my dad's transfer, Cigli had not yet built family housing. Dad went to Turkey while my mother, brother, and I moved to a small rental apartment in Brentwood, a suburb of Pittsburgh, not far from my mother's parents. Although I was too young to really understand the Cold War, I do remember feeling sad about my dad leaving.

"Where and what was Turkey," I remember asking, "and how long would he be gone?"

At last, base housing became available that fall, and our family and other military dependents were allowed to move to the tightly secured facility. While some families chose to stay at home in the states, my dad encouraged Peggy to come on yet another overseas adventure. We arrived surprised to see that our housing area was encircled with a barbed-wire fence to keep out the bands of gypsies and their camels who lived in surrounding camps.

THE LOUDEN FAMILY TRAVELS

A classic family photo in Izmir, Turkey, 1964.

It was a scary time, whether you lived at home or abroad. In the states, people were building bomb shelters, and school kids were taught to "duck and cover." In Columbus, my mother was the block captain for our local air-raid shelter. I can only imagine what she thought about moving to Turkey in the middle of a Cold War.

In Turkey, we had no television, and our news of the world consisted mainly of what we read in *The Stars and Stripes*, the worldwide military newspaper. On November 22, 1963, we received word through military channels that President Kennedy had been assassinated. Unlike people living in the states with access to 24-hour television and radio coverage, we had to wait for the story to unfold in bits and pieces. Meanwhile, as a major military installation overseeing missiles aimed at Russia, we felt isolated and vulnerable. Who had assassinated the President? Was it a communist conspiracy? Were we in danger? All we could do was wait. In the end, we were safe, and my parents continued to plan wonderful travel adventures to many different countries.

Despite our being on a remote and tightly secured base, every effort was made to provide fun and enjoyable activities to keep all the children and teens occupied. I remember fun times at the teen club, learning crafts like leather tooling, and, of course, the great military pastime of bowling. Another benefit of having no television access was that reading became a pleasurable pastime. Looking back, that was a wonderful gift. I remember reading *The Agony and The Ecstasy* prior to going to Rome and viewing Michelangelo's Sistine Chapel at the Vatican and his incredible David and The Pieta in Florence. An amazing experience I'll never forget!

Learning world history and culture in this way provided a special education. I learned how lucky I was to be an American and the very different status women had in other countries. My mom pointed out that as an American woman, I was free to receive a high level of education and to pursue whatever career or life pursuits I wanted. Today, I realize that my mother wanted me to have what she felt she had missed: options, opportunities, education, a career, and control over my life.

It was during Dad's duty at Cigli Air Base that our travels throughout the Middle East and Europe began in earnest. And what perfect timing: My brother and I were pre-teens who were studying world history in school.

Dad loved adventure and his cameras. He documented our travels with both movies and slide shows. No sound, however, this was, after all, in the days before video – yet what wonderful memories they bring back. We titled them "The Louden Family Travels," and we certainly did!

Living in Turkey was an amazing experience, although our base housing was basic at best. We lived in a tiny adobe dwelling. There was no grass, and there were no flowers in this hot, arid environment. But, we loved being there, as did the teachers who competed heavily to get this plum assignment. They knew that this location would afford them a rare opportunity

Kultur Park, Izmir, Turkey, July 1963.

to travel throughout the Middle East and Europe during Christmas and spring breaks, not to mention three months during summer.

As a result, I received some of the best years of my education delivered by great teachers on our base school. They also brought back treasures and history from their travels, making school fun and adventurous for me.

Just like the teachers who used the base in Turkey as a jump-off point for European and Middle Eastern travel, our family was ready to roam. As we toured all over Turkey, Europe, Egypt, and the Middle East, my parents encouraged us to read about the places we were about to see. Once we arrived at each new destination, we went on tours to learn about the local history.

On one amazing USO (United Service Organization) sponsored tour of the Middle East with my family, history came alive for me. It was an amazing itinerary.

We left the Izmir, Turkey, airport and traveled to Cairo, Egypt, soaring over the high mountains of Turkey and landing in the largest city of Africa, built on the east bank of the Nile. On the small island of Gezira, I watched as Arabian horses trotted around the polo grounds. At the old walled-in city of Babylon, I was amazed at seeing such poverty.

At the Egyptian Museum, I saw the treasures unearthed from King Tut's (Tutankhamen) tomb, including of all things, a chariot. The tomb was

Our USO tour at The Sphinx & The Great Pyramid of Khufu (Cheops).

accidentally discovered in 1917 and excavated in 1922; not for many decades, however, were its inner sanctum and the many jewels unearthed. It was amazing to learn that due to their belief in reincarnation, the Egyptian royalty were buried with not only all of their treasures but their servants as well. It certainly made me glad to be an American living in this century. Different cultures, different rituals, different times.

As American tourists, we were constantly approached by Egyptians, accomplished in the art of selling trinkets of all kinds, and looking for any change we could spare. But what really astounded me was that the majority of the throngs were barefoot children younger than myself. Here I was, staying at the Cairo Hilton, and yet, had I been born in Egypt, how different my life might have been. Talk about feeling blessed.

Of course, we visited the three Pyramids and the Sphinx. You can't imagine the immensity of these structures from photographs. They loom incredibly

Jim and Peg on their way to the Pyramids.

large above the sandy desert floor, miraculously and mysteriously engineered over 4,000 years ago.

The most memorable part of our trek was climbing to the summit of the largest of the Pyramids and the last remaining of the Seven Ancient Wonders of the World – The Great Pyramid of Khufu (Cheops). Built by King Kuhfu, also known by the Greek name "Cheops," the awesome structure stands nearly 455 feet high with a base that covers 13 square acres. It consists of approximately two million limestone and granite blocks weighing more than two tons each.

My "Big Jim" father hunched over to fit into the small inside passageway that led to the King's burial chamber. The stairwell was steep and narrow, allowing one line of tourists to go up and another to inch by us on their way down; it was stifling and crowded and not for anyone prone to claustrophobia.

We rode camels up a hill past the Pyramids; our caravan was 28-camels long, and I must tell you that the ride was definitely not as exotic as I thought it would be. The camels were smelly, particularly given the hot, still air. I knew this only too well. It was particularly unpleasant for me. Due to my small size, I rode upon a donkey, which placed me in close proximity to the rear-end of the camel in front of me, while the camel behind me loomed overhead with his large teeth and slobbery mouth.

134

Of course, since my brother was sitting on the hump of the camel to my rear, you can imagine that he was having a fun time watching his sister squirm.

We visited many mosques, including the huge and richly decorated Alabaster Mosque in Cairo, outfitted with expensive Persian rugs but no furniture. Rugs are necessary to accommodate kneeling Moslems, whose religion calls for prayers five times daily. Women were not allowed into the main mosque; instead, they were admitted into a back balcony. It was but one lesson where I found that women throughout much of the Third World are treated as second-class citizens.

I remembered hot summers in California and Pittsburgh, but they paled to the stifling heat in Egypt. We flew over the desert to Luxor, 275 miles south of Cairo, where our native guide told us he had never once seen rain. While visiting the Luxor Temple, I passed out from heat exhaustion. It's funny now to think back to those days before the proliferation of all of the many bottled waters. My guess is I passed out from dehydration.

Teri & King Ramses in Egypt.

Later, as we drove into the city along the Valley of the Nile, I saw entire villages constructed of mud huts. The road was lined with people, many carrying loads on their heads, some "wealthy" enough to ride little donkeys. A bridge was being rebuilt with the modern machinery of the day: shovels and hoes. In the city, we were treated to a horse-drawn carriage ride, traveling along dusty roads.

The Loudens on tour in Jerusalem, April 1964.

By contrast, we took a ferryboat across the Nile to encounter fertile valleys where sugar cane and hay grew in abundance. This "Valley of the Kings" was the site of the entombments, including King Tut's.

Next, we were off on a three-hour plane ride across the desert floor, where I spied camel caravans from the window of the plane. From whence they came and to where they were going remains a mystery for me... they were surrounded by miles and miles of sand.

We arrived in Jerusalem, where fields were green, buildings were modern, and new homes were sprouting on the outskirts. I suppose today those outskirts are considered the core of the town. And then we began to retrace the steps of Biblical history: Mt. Zion and the place of the Last Supper. We followed "the way of the Cross" with 14 stations marking where Jesus fell the first, second, and third times and where Simon of Cyreene was forced to bear the Cross for him. At the site of the crucifixion, there was a large statue of Jesus on the Cross, engulfed with candles, lights, and religious decorations.

A heavy wall of seven gates enclosed the old city of Jerusalem, and we entered through the Damascus Gate; this is the gate where Jesus made his triumphal march into Jerusalem. Later, at the Mount of Olives, the spot where Jesus ascended into heaven, we could look back to a panorama of the city.

I walked through the Garden of Gethsemane, where Jesus prayed below olive trees and where olive trees grow today. It was an inspiration to walk

through this garden and let my mind wander back to Biblical stories from my early childhood. I still cherish the Bible my parents bought me there with a beautiful cover of inlaid ivory and the word Jerusalem engraved on it.

Onward to Bethlehem, where I watched people working the fields with oxen and wooden plows as they must have done thousands of years ago. We stopped outside the city to visit the tomb of Rachel who died while giving birth to Benjamin.

Teri reflects near an ancient olive tree in the Garden of Gethsemane.

Louden Christmas greetings from Jerusalem.

The Church of the Nativity stands on the site of the inn where Mary and Joseph visited, and just inside was a manger.

We walked down narrow streets to the Wailing Wall, where Jesus came and wept for the city. Ironically, today it is illegal to cry or moan at the Wailing Wall.

Next we went "down" to Jericho, down to 800 feet below sea level, to stop at the Good Samaritan Inn, commemorating the tale of the Good Samaritan who was on his way to Jericho. Outside the city, I looked south to Mt. Nebo, where Moses led the children of Israel up to the Promised Land — the Jordan Valley, which looked rich and fertile.

But to the east, I saw a pitiful sight: a refugee camp of those who had been driven from their homes in Israel. Yes, this reminded me once more to remember to count my blessings.

Continuing downward, we went to the Dead Sea, 26 percent salt water and 1,200 feet below sea level. Close by is the place where the Dead Sea Scrolls were found. And upon our return trip to Jerusalem, we went up to Mt. Zion, and then to the site of the Last Supper.

Soon, we were on our way to Beirut, Lebanon, then one of the richest and most westernized cities in the Middle East. Sitting on the shore of the Mediterranean Sea, surrounded by St. Georges Bay and backed by the Lebanon Range, Beirut, with its many modern hotels and apartment buildings, appeared more stateside than any city I had seen since leaving Pittsburgh. My mom had heard of George's, a special custom jeweler in Beirut. George's was quite the talk among the other Air Force wives, and it was an amazing visit – there were more gems than I had seen in many museums. I now proudly wear some of the beautiful stone rings that my mom had had made there, along with the unique and intriguing Turkish puzzle ring my parents bought for me.

As we entered Syria, and its capital, Damascus, I noted that many people were dressed in old costumes. This was the only place where I saw women with veils completely covering their faces. They were wearing western clothing, high heels, and makeup (the veils were thin enough to see through) and yet here they were, shrouding their faces.

This trip was but one of the many Louden Family Travels made while we were stationed in Turkey. We traveled many times throughout Europe – visiting Paris and climbing the Eiffel Tower, visiting Venice where I was awestruck watching glassblowers making Venetian glass. From that time on, I've had a special appreciation for glass as art.

The Loudens visit Athens, Greece.

We had wonderful trips to Greece, attending Mardi Gras in Athens where everyone partied all night long, wearing masks of various political figures throughout the world. In those days, this included Nikita Khrushchev and President John F. Kennedy.

Of course, I would be remiss if I didn't mention all the amazing foods we tasted along the way. I didn't grow up with McDonald's® or Hostess Twinkies® Instead I developed a pallet for all types of international cuisines. I must say that when we finally did return to the states, the processed food was my biggest disappointment.

It was a misty and cool day when we visited Pompeii, Italy, and surveyed the ruins of a city that had been suddenly stilled when nearby Mt. Vesuvius erupted and suffocated the inhabitants in the year 79 AD. Eerily, they were captured in the last moments of their lives, as ash, a silent killer, like
carbon monoxide poisoning today, covered their bodies and preserved them for centuries. Later, armed with crooked walking sticks, and wearing raincoats, we climbed the slippery and rocky slopes of Vesuvius and gazed into the crater of the still-rumbling volcano. Another reminder of the fragility of life on earth.

Back to the good 'ole USA.

My family completed our tour of duty in Izmir by having the time of our lives traveling home on the luxurious ocean liner, The USS Independence.

It was an unforgettable experience with first-class accommodations, stops at scenic Italian ports, and meetings with interesting families and people from all over the world. The ship featured a state-of-the-art movie theatre where we watched the first James Bond thriller: Goldfinger. My brother and I thought we were really cool.

As we entered New York City Harbor, I had tears in my eyes as we sailed past the Statue of Liberty, a symbol of our nation's freedom. While we loved our overseas adventures, it was time to come home to the good 'ole USA.

World's Fair, New York, 1964.

The World's Fair was on in New York City, and what a thrill to have that be our first stop after years of being outside America. That's where Dad saw the first model of the new 1965 Ford Mustang. Not surprisingly, he ordered one of the first Mustangs off the assembly line; it was red, and red-hot, and would soon find a home in Cheyenne, Wyoming, Dad's next duty station.

When we got the Cheyenne assignment, my mother was anticipating the worst. There was always anxiety in the military with the question, "Where in the world are we going next?" She was imagining a hick cowboy town, that she would be cast as the Western pioneer wife and mother. How would she stay down on this farm after she'd seen Paree?

But Francis E. Warren Air Force Base and Cheyenne were actually a fabulous surprise. Base housing turned out to be a grand home with fireplaces in every room, high ceilings, floor to ceiling windows, and large claw-foot bathtubs. My brother's accommodations consisted of the entire top floor of our four-story home, which he loved; it was his private quarters, a thrill for a teenage boy.

It was the best and grandest home we ever lived in, except perhaps our Japanese mansion where my mother had had the added bonus of housekeepers, gardeners, and cooks. In Cheyenne, we experienced the Wild, Wild West, riding horses and enjoying Cheyenne Frontier Days, the biggest rodeo in the country. And we definitely experienced the four seasons of the year: In the winter, J.L. and I built snowmen and had snowball fights. In the summer, we experienced hot and dry winds and watched an endless supply of those tumbling tumbleweeds tumble across our front yard.

One particularly memorable trip was to nearby Colorado Springs and the Air Force Academy. The Academy's Chapel is an architecturally beautiful structure with striking stain-glass windows. I'll never forget the emotion of singing the Air Force Hymn, *Lord, Guard and Guide the Men Who Fly*, in this very special place.

As much as we all liked Cheyenne, once again the military had big plans for "Big Jim." It was 1966, and the Vietnam War was now raging. Pope Air Force Base in Fayetteville, North Carolina, was looking for C-130 pilots and Dad was tapped.

Pope was located in the middle of Ft. Bragg, a massive army reservation and post, if not the largest in the country. It was military central during the Vietnam War, and I have some emotional memories from these days. Many of our military friends and neighbors left for the war, and we never knew who would return. Our church was the Ft. Bragg Main Post Army Chapel — together we prayed for the safe return of our troops. When my dad went to fly in Vietnam, I was old enough to understand the potential danger, and you can bet I said my share of prayers for him. It was a special reunion when he returned.

There was no base housing so we rented a home near the base. It had been a long time since I had not lived on an Air Force base, and I missed the sense of community that came with living on base and in close proximity to other military families. Although I didn't know it at the time, Fayetteville, North Carolina, would be our last move as a family. In fact, it would prove to be my parents' home for the next 35 years and the first place where they actually bought a house.

★

PEGGY'S ROOTS

"If you look up, you will miss it. If you look back, you will be scared. Don't be afraid, just take my hand."

— Jean Pierre Marques

Every American military family will recognize that behind every successful career officer is a supportive spouse. When military personnel go to war or to duty stations at remote locations, greater demands are placed upon the wives, or in today's military, the increasing number of husbands left behind as well. It's the spouse who must assume the position of head of family, run the household, and function independently. And they typically assume the responsibility for planning and executing the many relocations that take place throughout a military person's career.

In my upbringing, this fell heavily on the wives, as is still true today. This chapter is not only a tribute to my mother, Peggy, but also a tribute to all military spouses… and to their children.

These thoughts come from my heart and from years living with, talking to, and listening to my mother. I started this book ten years after her passing. Unfortunately, I did not have the benefit of the in-depth personal interviews that I conducted with my father as part of my research. But writing this story allowed me to finally take time to reflect and understand the mysteries of my mother and the impact she had on my life.

Early in their marriage, Peggy had refused to accompany my father in some of his far-flung assignments. Time changed that as their love grew and my brother and I came into the world. Once hooked, however — and a major part of that hook was the unique and luxurious lifestyle that came with living in a Japanese mansion — Peggy adapted well to a life of continual change.

My mother evolved into the perfect military wife. She was, in essence, the best soldier my dad could have found. Each time Dad received orders to report to a new base, off he went in advance of the family; my mother brought up the rear, charged with the workload of closing down one household and opening up the next. She was the one who planned and managed every detail of our physical moves while my brother and I helped with the execution.

Margaret (Peggy) Neuner was born January 11, 1921, in Pittsburgh, Pennsylvania, the daughter of two proud, albeit poor, German immigrants.

Peggy's dad at work in the German Beneficial Union (GBU) bar in Pittsburgh, 1957.

Her dad John was a bartender, and her mother Minnie worked in a bakery. They eventually bought a home in Brentwood Borough where they lived their entire lives. In contrast to the military, the Neuners' life experiences were simple yet stable.

Mom's family lived on a shoestring budget. I remember well my mother's stories about their first house with its dirt floors. She told us about their Depression-era desserts — once a week, they could look forward to a small bag of gingersnap surprises. My grandmother would mash yellow food coloring into lard so it would look like butter; it's no wonder I never saw my mom spread butter or margarine on her bread!

My mother was intelligent, street-smart, and the consummate lady. Despite her modest family upbringing, Pittsburgh was quite the cosmopolitan city, filled with old steel and railroad money. The family would get all dressed up, take the streetcars downtown, and look at the latest fashions in the elegant department stores of those days: Horne's, Gimbel's, and Kaufman's. Mom quickly developed a knack for putting together the right dress, shoes, purse, and makeup. Of course, women in the 1950s always dressed for their men, but Mom dressed to the nines whether walking with a stroller, preparing dinner for the family, or hosting the many cocktail and dinner parties at our home. She wore high heels for all activities.

One of many mess-dress formals.

To succeed in business, my wardrobe took on a much different look. When Booz, Allen & Hamilton, a leading international management consulting firm, hired me in 1979, it hosted John Malloy, author of Dress for Success in a presentation to the executives. Men were to wear white shirts, Brooks Brothers suits, and beige raincoats; the few professional women in the firm at the time were "highly encouraged" to adapt the same look, and I began wearing blue, gray, and black suits with white cotton shirts and pearls; quite a contrast to my mother's beautiful pink coats, Japanese silk suits, and white organza blouses.

147

My mom told me how much she would have liked to have gone to college, but in her era, most women were not directed towards higher education. Her parents saved long and hard and did manage to send her brother, Johnny, to Pittsburgh University. Their dad took on extra jobs, but it was well worth it when graduation day came for Johnny with a college degree as an aeronautical engineer. Ironically, his first job was at Glenn L. Martin Corporation where he helped design the B-26 Marauder that my dad flew in WWII.

Her sentiments on education stirred within me at an early age — I would go to college and figure out how to pay for it myself if I had to. And I did, with scholarships and odd jobs as a grocery checker and grading papers in the N.C. State math department. I earned not just one degree, but two, a bachelor's in applied mathematics and an MBA. I believe Mom lived vicariously through my college and business-world experiences, and helped spur me on as I pursued my education and business career.

I am convinced that military children either thrive in the dynamic, constantly changing environment of military life, or they come to resent it. This could also be said for the spouses. In my mother's case, it was a love-hate relationship; perhaps I should say hate-love, since she grew to love it. While she grew to love the adventure and world travel, she did not enjoy the constant moving and upheaval of family and home. But she accepted it all as her commitment to be a supportive wife and mother.

My brother, J.L., and I were polar opposites in our response to "the life." Perhaps it was as a result of the circumstances that surrounded my family when we were born, just three years apart, but light-years away in our parents' circumstances.

My brother, conceived just six months following my father's plane crash, was born August 28, 1950. Amazing, but true: passion, apparently, can overcome physical adversity and pain.

My brother was born at a time when my mother was consumed with worry about her husband and his rehabilitation. When Dad was transferred to the hospital in Arkansas, and then to Walter Reed in Washington, D.C., my mother was on her own. Although Dad eventually was released and lived at home, he was focused on his recovery and rehabilitation and required my mother's energy and comfort throughout her pregnancy and my brother's first two months.

J.L. was born at Walter Reed Army Medical Center, the same hospital that my mother visited daily as my father healed. Dad recalls she was "always there," occupying herself with reading, often from *Baby and Child Care*, while she quietly encouraged his recovery. This 1946 book by Dr. Spock became the "bible" for many post-war brides; the stained and dog-eared volume that accompanied us throughout the world was her guiding light into child rearing.

My mother had no family network nearby to support her entry into motherhood. She had to figure out how to make baby formula and properly heat the glass bottles in boiling water.

Circumstances were much improved when I entered the world at a tiny 5 pounds, 13 ounces. My family was living in a gorgeous Japanese mansion in Nagoya. In 1953, the wealthy Japanese, still recovering from the financial

Peggy and Teri in Nagoya, Japan.

One-year-old Teri with her nursemaid Kuni-Son in Nagoya, Japan.

ravages of World War II, were pleased to rent out their beautiful mansions.

This time around, my mother had the services of a wonderful, trained nursemaid; Kuni-Son was a bright university student. I was blessed with 24-hour nurturing and unconditional love of "two mothers" 24 hours a day.

A household of helpers — maids and cooks and gardeners and nursemaids — supported my mother, and she was able to focus on nurturing her new baby and three-year-old son.

Mom also had a network of military wives and mothers, and together they could share laughs and child-raising tips in this far-away place. My dad was healed and happy and once more serving his country as a pilot during wartime, this time in the Korean War.

My brother J.L. never embraced the constant, changing life of military travel. As an adult, he settled in Charlotte, North Carolina, to a life with minimal change, more grounded than my world of continuous travel and relocation. Today, he has a successful dental practice and is the father of my nephew Les, James. L. Louden, III.

J.L. later told me that our father's absence during tours of duty probably affected him, as a son, more than it did me, as a daughter. Dad wasn't able to be there for many of those special father-son events like Little League

Proud mom & dad with just baptized Teri and little J.L., Sept. 1953.

games or Boy Scout troop meetings. But, although my brother and I had different reactions to military life, the good news is that both of us are content today and appreciate and enjoy the unique life directions we each have taken. I can understand his life choices and the different ways we responded to a life of constant moving and upheaval.

The military lifestyle also taught me to embrace diversity. When we were stationed at Cigli Air Base in Izmir, Turkey, I remember the wonderful experience of getting to know Turkish families. The women were so talented in many ways, and they gave us beautiful handmade gifts: luxurious knit sweaters and silver jewelry. My best friend, Ethel, was African-American and my partner in the children's choir. Walking down the aisle each Sunday in the base chapel, we sang at the top of our lungs and giggled together as we surveyed the church audience and examined their faces.

Friendships seem to form thick and fast among military dependents, even those who meet later in life. Today, one of my dearest friends, Linda Burns, is also the daughter of a career Air Force pilot. We met while working in Chicago and felt an immediate bond as we compared notes on our military upbringing and pilot dads. One also learns early on in a military family that friendships can continue even when families are transferred away.

Mom never lost her gift for entertaining.

Today, Linda lives in Boston, and I'm at the other end of the country in San Diego. But through calls, letters, e-mails, and occasional visits, we've maintained a close friendship.

You learn in the military to work at friendships; and part of that is the art of entertainment. My mother was a perfect wife and hostess. Like many women in her generation, she spent her time cooking, cleaning, and nurturing, rather than working outside the home. It was part of every officer wife's duty to entertain, and Mom was certainly the "Hostess with the Mostess." My brother and I were participants in the social scene as well; each week I tagged along as Mom did her grocery shopping at the commissary, and I learned to make appetizers and aided in dinner preparations. My brother and I helped serve and clean up after the dinners. Mom's great organizational skills in party planning, not just the food, but flowers, music, and timing, became a solid foundation for my future hosting of executive parties and parties for friends. Mom taught me at an early age not only how to host a party, but also to be able to enjoy it as well.

On Sundays, my mom planned our weekly menus followed by the necessary grocery shopping items. The four food groups were a way of life at all meals. As children of the Depression, my parents enforced the eat-every-thing-on-your-plate-and-be-grateful-for-it philosophy. It was never a question of what we liked; we listened and followed their rules. But the food was always delicious, albeit starchy; our home was a shining example of the era's love affair with casseroles that allowed frugal families to stretch their food budgets. Mom and the other military wives loved sharing recipes and even had a self-published cookbook they all contributed to, the Military Wife's Casserole Cookbook. The cookbook included their names, duty stations, and recipes for such specialties as ham-Sparta casserole, tuna noodle casserole with onion rings on top, a Mexican casserole with corn chips, and, the ever-popular Spam® and apples.

Along with the rest of the family, Mom enjoyed the bowling leagues, which are part of most military family social scenes. She tried her hand at golf, but eventually left this pastime to my dad. As with most officers, the golf course (and the 19th hole) played a major part of Dad's social life.

Jim bowls a near perfect game, 1967.

In contrast to the parties and fun times, there were the times my mom spent worrying about my dad and our family. Her number-one priority was her family's needs over her own happiness; she was the detail person who made sure everything ran efficiently for all of us. For every one time he didn't worry, she worried two.

From a very young age, I also worried about Dad's safety every time he flew. In base chapels, we would pray for the safe return of the airmen. I can recall singing with tears in my eyes the official hymn of the US Air Force:

Lord, Guard and Guide the Men Who Fly

Lord, guard and guide the men who fly
Through the great spaces of the sky;
Be with them traversing the air
In darkening storms or sunshine fair.

Thou who dost keep with tender might
The balanced birds in all their flight,

Thou of the tempered winds, be near,
That, having Thee, they know no fear.
Control their minds with instinct fit
What time, adventuring, they quit
The firm security of land;
Grant steadfast eye and skillful hand.

Aloft in solitudes of space,
Uphold them with Thy saving grace.
O God, protect the men who fly
Thru lonely ways beneath the sky. Amen.

It was always a thrill to see Dad walk through the door after a flight. I can still remember his flight suit, filled with the smells of the cockpit – grease and diesel and metal and leather I suppose, but to me it was all manly and Dad. And upon each return, I'd eagerly scramble to open the many zippered pockets on that flight suit to find the surprises he had hidden there for me.

I believe when military families pull up stakes and move every two years, parents become the one constant in a child's life; peer pressure is lessoned because peers come and go. I feel blessed to have had a life of change as part of my upbringing, as it prepared me for the business world, where for many people, change creates stress. I came to view change as part of the adventure and excitement of life rather than something to avoid or stress over. After all, change is the one constant we can all count on.

My mother's stress with the constant change was different from mine. As I interviewed my dad to study our life for the first time, I began to think about what her life must have been like as she supported and tried to keep up with "Big Jim."

When the men came back after World War II, couples were eagerly marrying, settling down, and having children; just like Ward and June Cleaver on "Leave it to Beaver." And yet, by today's standards, these couples, my parents included, hardly knew each other before they married.

My father's courtship of my mother began in earnest when my dad returned to Pittsburgh after the war in October 1945. Dating consisted of evenings on her parents' porch, with one or both of her parents always present, an occasional movie, and dancing to one of the Big Bands. Three months later, my parents married. They honeymooned in Niagara Falls in the midst of a blinding snowstorm. Mom ribbed Dad about this for years.

No doubt my mother expected they would settle down in Pittsburgh for the rest of their lives, riding streetcars and buying cakes and other goodies from the famous Dudtz German Bakery. I'm certain Mom had no idea of the likes of a PX, Commissary, or Class 6 store.

My father was head of the family and his wife steadfastly supported him. Dad made every major decision while my mother decided and executed the day-to-day details. After we were born, I think Mom saw the writing on the wall. Dad was a military man, and we were a military family. End of debate. On with the game.

In October 1952, Dad was scheduled to go to combat in Korea. As a farewell, he took my mom to the San Francisco Bay area before her return to Pittsburgh, Pennsylvania, to stay with her parents to wait for his return. The night before his departure, they made love, and I was conceived, coincidentally, in the small town of Pittsburg, California.

Dad was originally scheduled for combat duty. But upon his arrival overseas, he met up with an officer in charge of assigning Public Information Officers for the Far East. Upon learning of his prior Air Force public information assignments, he reassigned Dad to be the Public Information Officer for the Japan Air Defense Force in Nagoya. This enabled his family to join him overseas, yet another of those positive coincidences in Dad's life.

And so Peggy Louden, now pregnant with me and with a two-year-old in tow, prepared for a major move overseas. She boarded a ship with trepidation and began the long trip to Japan. It was her first time off the continent.

I can only imagine what my mom's state-of-mind must have been. This young mother and mother-to-be had just spent months nursing my father back to health. She had morning sickness and was headed to a foreign country while a war raged on in nearby Korea. She had no idea what life would be like when she arrived. She must have been guided by a tremendous love for my father and the faith that the Good Lord would guide them through it smoothly.

Kanko Hotel in Nagoya, Japan. Jim & Peggy, left, with military friends, 1953.

Peggy and J.L. shopping in Nagoya, Japan.

F-94 formation & beautiful Mt. Fuji.

But fate had a dose of good fortune in store for little Peggy. The tour of duty in Japan was no less than fabulous. Upon arrival, she found my dad had negotiated to live on a beautiful Japanese estate complete with full Japanese gardens and a staff of servants. Mom joined in the many social activities at the Officers' Club in Nagoya, and for the next five years developed a network of close friends among the military wives.

Following the conclusion of the Korean War in 1953, my parents took time to travel throughout Japan visiting Tokyo, Kyoto, and Mt. Fuji. Dad shot rolls of 16-millimeter film, creating our own family documentary of the history of post-World War II Japan.

My mother always fondly recalled their long tour of duty in Japan. This experience began her own form of traveling education, learning about other cultures and the history of the world. She had lived a charmed life in the Far East, my dad's crash forgotten or deeply buried in her mind.

It had been the first time since their marriage that my mother had time to play, freed up from traditional household duties and caregiving for my dad. In one respect, world travel became my mother's college education, and she thrived on it.

Aah, but all good things must come to an end, and five years later the Air Force called Dad back from Japan to the homeland for a new tour of duty at March Air Force Base in Riverside, California. I entered kindergarten right after we arrived, and learned quickly the need for making new friends. Gone were the housekeepers, cooks, nursemaids, and the Japanese mansion for my mother. Our new home was small and a train ran in the gully behind, tooting all day long; not quite the grandeur of the Japanese mansion or the serenity of its gardens.

This would begin a series of moves that would take place throughout my dad's Air Force career as he accepted different assignments, flew new planes, or supervised missile sites. My brother and I helped my mom prepare for the moves and the always-painful process of unpacking and resettling in as short a time as possible. We never owned a house while I was growing up, as base housing or what was available was provided for us.

With each move, Mom had an uncanny knack of managing to fit all our household goods into each place, adding the right curtains — the old ones never seemed to fit — and hanging artwork. To me, every place we lived was my special home. Like so many military families that had experienced international tours of duty, our home contained wonderful accessories from our world travels.

It was only natural that I followed suit. My own home has items I've collected from the many cities where I've traveled and lived both in this country and abroad. I continue to feel that every home is special, not only because of my things but also because these items evoke memories of wonderful friendships I've made in each place I've lived. This ability to move and always feel at home is an awesome gift that my parents, and particularly my mom, passed on to me.

There's a saying that home is where the heart is; that's what my mom always taught me. We'd move and we'd celebrate; the friends we had made would stay within our hearts, and we'd take wing to new adventures that lay ahead.

Throughout my life, I've branched out to new cities and new ventures, and it was always possible because I had strong roots that were grounded in love.

PEGGY'S WINGS

*"There are three words that sweetly blend, and on
the heart are graven. A precious, soothing balm they lend,
they are 'mother,' home and heaven."*

— Anonymous

My parents' last assignment was Fayetteville, North Carolina, where they retired and lived for more than 35 years, the longest time they lived in one place together.

Fayetteville was a hot spot when we moved there. The Vietnam War was on and at the heart of the city was Fort Bragg, the largest U.S. army post at that time and home to the Green Berets, the Army Special Forces known for their hardcore training.

Dad was stationed at Pope Air Force Base, home of the 43rd Air Wing, with the slogan "We put the air in airborne;" it was a small footprint in the middle of the massive Fort Bragg Military Reservation.

Pope was the first base where Dad was stationed that was more than just an Air Force base. We learned firsthand about the Army and ground vs. air warfare. As we drove through Fort Bragg to get to Pope, we passed many Army tanks and jeeps. It was strange to see everyone wearing Army khakis and camouflage instead of the Air Force dress blue I was used to. We made many friends among the Army troops, and I came to appreciate the common bond among all branches of the military.

In 1968, at age 17, I took a job to earn money for college as a cashier in a "shoppette," one of the many small beer and sundries stores on the post. It turned out to be quite the experience. The building was a Quonset hut, made out of corrugated metal. This low-tech building didn't have air conditioning, and it wasn't the most fun place to be throughout a sultry North Carolina summer. Handling the heat was only a small part of my learning experience. I became exposed to a brave new world of vocabulary filled with colorful language and the never-ending litany of expletives uttered from hundreds of GIs and reservists who made their way into the hut for beers and smokes and magazines. Eventually, I didn't even blush when they stood in front of me, purchasing the latest issue of *Playboy*, ogling the centerfold with one hand, the other outstretched to receive their change.

My brother left for college at the end of that summer. My parents were proud that he picked Penn State, honoring their Pennsylvania heritage. They relished going up to Penn State football games and seeing that famous coach, Joe Paterno, at work. While my brother enjoyed Penn State, when it came my turn to choose a college, I picked North Carolina State. I wanted to avoid my brother's experiences of trudging across a snow-covered campus in the middle of those cold Pennsylvania winters.

My mother had been very emotional when J.L. left for college. The "empty nest" days were beginning, and she knew I would be off three years later. In the meantime, she was occupied with and devoted to her father's welfare. My grandmother, a diabetic, had passed away in her early 60s. Following her death, my grandfather, whom we affectionately called Pappap Johnny, had lived alone in Pittsburgh. But by the time he reached his mid-70s and needed a cane to get around, Mother encouraged him to move in with us. He would be far safer in our home, where there were fewer steps to climb, and no snow and ice. Pappap lived with us for nearly five years, and both my brother and I enjoyed his lovable personality. He bonded with our miniature dachshund, Pretzel, and walked her slowly around the block every day for his exercise.

Pappap, like my dad, was a wonderful father, and we loved him dearly. Eventually, we turned to a nursing home for that extra care that was so crucial in his final days. My mom visited him almost every day. This was

Pappap Johnny celebrates his 87th with Peggy & Teri.

another great example of a wonderful father-daughter bonding, as my mother adored her dad, and it gave her great pleasure to care for him in his final years. I remember how very sad she was when he died in 1972.

At last, it was college time for Teri. I remember my parents driving me from Fayetteville to North Carolina State University in Raleigh. We unloaded my few worldly possessions that barely fit into the tiny dorm room along with my roommate and all her worldly possessions as well. I was so excited and loved the thought of freedom and independence. My dad, also an independent spirit, was excited for me as I entered into this new chapter of my life. But my mother had a harder time; after much sobbing and hugging, my dad pulled her away and they left. Peggy was once again off to care for just one person… "Big Jim."

It was a difficult time for my mother who, up to this point in her life, devoted herself to her family. My dad had started his new career in real estate that kept him active and fueled his passion of being with and helping people. Mother was lonely; she needed something to replace the lost excitement of traveling the world, nurturing her children, and caring for her father in his final years.

Peggy and Jim in Seville, Spain, 1979.

An underground church's amazing organ pipes. Oslo, Norway, 1989.

It is ironic that the woman who had resisted moving and change so much eventually grew to thrive and depend on it. When travel and moving ceased, and her children left, she didn't know how to create that same energy in her new life. Mom gradually grew into a state of quiet acceptance as she waited for my dad to take the lead.

Finally, when he retired from real estate, they were free to travel and travel they did – 33 Elder Hostels and a life on the road of adventure; Mom rebounded. My dad's retirement and their travel adventure planning happened around the same time as their 40th wedding anniversary. There was a major party at the Fort Bragg Officers' Club with hundreds of friends. I flew in from Chicago; my brother came from Charlotte, and even my dad's sister, Aunt Jean, drove up from Florida. In true military style, Dad's buddies got together and gave him a surprise present that evening – a beautiful model of the B-26 Martin Marauder he had flown in WWII.

Peggy and Jim traveling on the Repin Train from Helsinki to Leningrad, 1987.

Today, Dad still proudly displays this on his coffee table. That day, even though she had been the one who spent many months planning for the perfect anniversary party, my mom didn't get a gift from the guys. Even on their 40th wedding anniversary, Dad held the spotlight, and she was the good soldier.

But alas, it was on one of their many trips, in October 1992, that Mom began exhibiting major symptoms of the neuroblastoma brain tumor that would eventually take her life. Earlier indications started showing up when she often misplaced her keys, could not find her purse, and then, most tellingly, forgot how to tie her shoes.

My parents contacted me for guidance. With my career in the medical field, I knew something serious was up and directed her to immediately seek a diagnosis. A CAT scan disclosed a tumor the size of a peach; Mom was given nine months to live.

Faced with this devastating diagnosis, we then had to decide on a course of treatment. The surgeon, of course, said, "Operate," and Mom and Dad thought that was the way to go because their generation grew up totally relying on their physician's every word. I, however, spoke to a medical oncologist at Duke University and discovered that it was unlikely that surgery would prolong Mom's life enough to justify the risks. With surgery, there was a probability she could wake up with severe brain damage and spend the rest of her days in a nursing home.

Instead, we elected to have Mom undergo chemotherapy and radiation; she wanted it because it gave her, and my dad, hope. In the early weeks following her diagnosis, both my dad and mom were, I believe, in a state of denial, not uncommon when someone has been handed a death sentence, so to speak. However, after the therapy had been completed, X-rays showed there had been no reduction in the tumor; the cancer was continuing to grow. By December, denial moved into acceptance.

And that's when Mom began to exhibit the fortitude and strength that had been her signature earlier in life. She persevered through a life of constant moves, my dad's injury and gradual recovery, and countless deaths including some sudden and tragic air fatalities of Dad's fellow pilots.

Much more so than civilian life, the military life prepares you to face and prepare for the reality of death. My mother was a wonderful example of this training. Once her diagnosis was clear, she lived as full a life as possible. She traveled as long as she could with my dad.

At a large New Year's party my father held in her honor, she was the center of attention; she ate whatever she wanted, whenever she wanted, and was openly happy and positive. Dad had invited more than 100 friends who were delighted to share in this special day. It was a wonderful time for all of her friends to share their love with her, while she was still cognizant, and to say goodbye – until we meet again.

Teri brings mom her comforting "furry friends." —photo by Cramer Gallimore, cgphoto.com

On one visit, I brought my two miniature, longhair dachshunds, Honey and Angel, to share with her the unconditional love that is so special with animals. They sensed immediately her need of attention, curling up on her lap at all times. She loved petting them.

It was also touching to see my dad assume the role of caregiver that had always been her duty. He knew it was his time and rose to the occasion as best as he knew how. With hospice care and wonderful "angel" caregivers like Becky Canady, for whom my dad and I will forever be grateful, my mother was comfortably cared for throughout her final months in her own home.

How could I ease my mother's suffering? What could I give her? Do for her? I had brought down my little dachshunds that were full of unconditional love. Then it occurred to me how highly she regarded her Penn State hero, Football Coach Joe Paterno. How could I get him to call or write her?

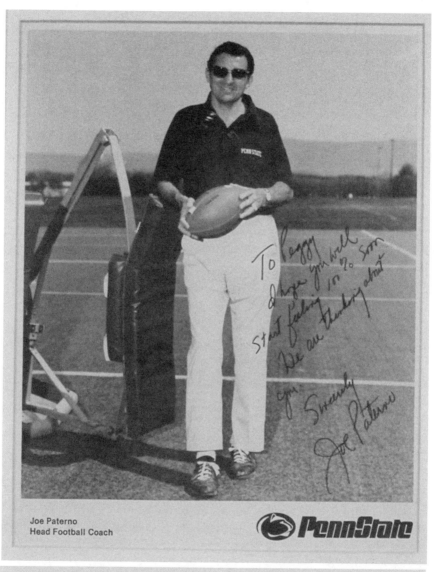

Joe Paterno
Head Football Coach

Joe Paterno, Penn State Head Football Coach.

I put it on my to-do list.

During this stressful time, I was attending a medical conference in Washington, D.C. As I came out of a lecture and down the stairs toward the hotel lobby, I stared in amazement — Joe Paterno was standing there in the lobby. It was one of those "On God's Wings" coincidences that I will always be grateful for. I ran up to him and explained the medical situation of one of his biggest fans — native Pittsburgher Peggy Louden. He handed me his business card and asked me to contact him by mail.

Unbeknownst to my parents, I wrote a letter to him restating how my mom held him in such high esteem. He shortly responded with a color autographed photograph inscribed, "To Peggy, I hope you will start feeling 100 percent soon. We are thinking about you." Sincerely, Joe Paterno.

Dad framed and hung Joe's photo on the wall where Mom could see it, and it thrilled her and uplifted her spirits through her final days. I will always be grateful to Joe Paterno for his thoughtfulness.

One evening, Mom and I were sitting at the kitchen table. She wore her little sailor hat to cover her hair loss from the chemotherapy. She looked at me and smiled that adorable smile of hers. Mom had always been petite, but now she looked so frail; this night she looked almost childlike as she smiled at me with laughter in her eyes.

It was then that I lost my composure; it hit me hard that soon she would no longer be with us. My heart took over, and I began to sob. She hugged me tightly, but that only made me weep more.

I will never forget the profound moment when she asked very simply, "Why are you crying, my love?"

Not in control of my typical logical self, I found myself blurting out, "Mom, you're going to die. I can't fathom how to live without you here with me. What will I do without you?" I had lost control and was mad at myself for thinking of myself first, which made me cry all the harder.

Her response pierced my heart and soul. "Yes, my person will be gone shortly," she said firmly. "Moreover, my child, you too will pass when your time has come. However, my soul will be with you always, and your soul too will last forever; so you need not worry. Just make sure that every moment of your time on this earth today is spent as you desire, that you help others, and you are happy each day and every moment."

Her thoughts were not of her pending demise, but focused on her daughter's happiness. She was the loving caretaker she had always been, that wise and spiritual soul, profound teacher, and role model.

Her words struck a cord within me, her workaholic daughter who rarely found time for relaxation and enjoyment of life's simple pleasures. In her last moments of life on this earth, she thought not of herself but of helping me navigate my future.

I began to think differently about my life after my mother's passing. I started to realize that there was more to life than achievement in work and financial success. My mother's lesson was to follow my heart's desires, not dictated by the outside world.

Mom proved that love and great street smarts always win in the end. Mom, I will love and give thanks always for your wonderful gifts and wisdom.

It would be a long hard road for me to change and begin to bring more balance into my life. Writing this book and learning from my dad provided wonderful encouragement, but I think the seed was planted when I lost my mother.

ON GOD'S *WINGS*

My mother died on March 3, 1993.

I was in the middle of leading a four-day executive retreat in Chicago when the call came from my dad. Our group took a recess, and the executives encouraged me to cancel the remainder of our session. But I knew they had traveled from other cities to attend, and we had too much to do in too short a time. And I heard a voice, my mother's, telling me to continue with the conference: It is what she would have wanted. Inspired by her strength, I was able to continue. When I returned home that night, the tears flowed.

Mom's service was held at our church, the Main Post Chapel at Fort Bragg in North Carolina. The chapel was packed; Mother had so many friends, and Dad's friends were there to support him as well. After it was over, my dad, brother, and I drove to Washington, D.C. for a final touching ceremony.

My mother's ashes are kept at Arlington National Cemetery; one day my father's will rest next to hers. They both were honored to know that even after their lives, they would be in the company of military men and women who had served their country well.

Throughout the church service and internment at Arlington, Dad was sad but composed. He said he would never marry again, as he would always be married to Peggy, and years later he is still the happy, independent bachelor. But he would carry on with his travels and love of people; he would always be the "Hubba Dubba Man."

And me? Work helped me keep my mind off grieving, but I do believe that it is right and it is strengthening to allow ourselves times to remember and reflect. For me, those times often come when I am flying from one destination to another. As I sit in the plane, I look out to the white clouds and wondrous blue sky and feel my mother's presence, *On God's Wings.*

PEGGY'S WINGS

Anyone who knows me will tell you that I am my father's daughter, following in his footsteps, loving life and its constant change and adventure with a positive attitude. I probably would have become an Air Force pilot myself if it had been possible when I graduated in the '70s. My dad supported the premise that I could be and could do anything I wanted in life, and he always told me to follow my dreams. He encouraged me to be mentally and physically strong, which spurred my love of reading and physical exercise. He gave me a level of self-confidence that has served me well in all aspects of my life. The way a father communicates with and relates to his daughter has a huge impact on her self-image and self-esteem.

My mother, God bless her, gave me the solid roots of family stability and love and, like my dad, encouraged my independence and capabilities.

I am so grateful to each of them for these gifts.

My mother often summed up how my brother and I were raised, "We give our children roots, and we give our children wings."

FULL THROTTLE INTO RETIREMENT

*"We are each of us angels with only one wing.
And we can only fly by embracing each other."*

— Luciano De Crescenzo

With his retirement from the Air Force in 1971, Jim, now 50, had time on his hands. He was too young and active to retire. As he transitioned from military to civilian life, he knew he had to keep a link to flying and the military in some form or another. It was in his blood, and he wanted to maintain the military connection.

He played golf for a few months, but eventually grew bored with it. Days on the links with his buddies did, however, spark the idea to pursue a second career in real estate.

That October, he passed the state board and became a licensed real estate broker. Real estate gave him a vehicle to connect with his military buddies, build a new career, and be constantly on the go.

He started selling real estate with a good friend, Dave Lain, a retired Army Lieutenant Colonel. Dave taught Jim how to list and appraise houses. A short time later, Jim formed an exclusive partnership with John Koenig, a homebuilder. Jim's real estate career lasted 15 years until his retirement.

Retirement means different things to different people. For Jim, it meant he had more opportunities to be of service — to his church, his community, and his veteran community. His love of life and people spurred him to further his interests and develop other ways of giving back.

Active in many causes in his hometown of Fayetteville, North Carolina, he volunteered every Friday morning in the Retiree Affairs Office at Pope Air Force Base. He read the Fayetteville Observer newspaper to more than 400 blind people over Fayetteville State University's radio station.

Embracing new friends.

He was a member of the Alliance Club for the Blind, the Lions Club, and a Shriner.

Every Sunday morning, you could find Jim at the Fort Bragg Main Post Chapel in Fayetteville, ushering and greeting members and visitors, and reading from the Bible in the pulpit.

Jim suffered lingering back problems, and he worked out three or four times a week at the local YMCA. And always, he maintained a positive mental attitude, never forgetting to appreciate what he had by the grace of God: his life.

After Peggy's death in 1993, Jim pushed himself onward. He missed her deeply, but somehow was able to handle his sorrow by thinking not of himself, but of others. And Jim was always going somewhere. Peggy's death did not slow Jim Louden down. Probably, nothing could. He was aware of

Taj Mahal. Agra, India.

a number of men who floundered after losing their wives, but his positive attitude kept him in motion.

Often, Dad told me, he dreams of Peggy accompanying him on his travels. Peggy is obviously with him in spirit.

He continued with his volunteer work and traveled on the road, in the air, and on the seas. He traveled the world visiting more than 50 countries and all seven continents following Peggy's death. In South America, he rode on a skiff and lodged in a hotel just 200 steps above the Amazon River. He surveyed herds of antelope, elephants, and zebras and spied a lion while riding the Blue Train from Pretoria to Capetown, South Africa. On a cruise to Antarctica, Jim joined the penguins on the frozen ice. He walked the Great Wall of China and visited India's Taj Mahal. Dad has made more than a dozen ocean voyages to places like Bali, the Greek Islands, and Singapore.

Coast Guard Cadets, Bermuda.

Antarctica.

Riding The Orient Express.

Nyeri, Kenya.

Shanghai, China.

Dunedin, New Zealand.

Featherdale Wildlife Park, Sydney, Australia.

Hale Koa Hotel swimming pool, Hawaii, 1995.

Aloha from Hawaii.

Tower Bridge, London.

American cemetery, Omaha Beach, Normandy.

WWII Bomb Group Reunion, 1976.

Enjoying Kansas City jazz at dad's 397th WWII Bomb Group reunion, 1997.

In 1995, he went to England as a guest at the groundbreaking for the American Air Museum at Duxford Air Station. He also visited France where finally, he set foot on the ground he'd only seen from the air in World War II. Taking a bus from Paris to Normandy, he walked through the American cemetery at Omaha Beach. While looking at the crosses, tears streamed down his face, as he thought of the boys in the boats he had seen from his B-26 Martin Marauder on D-Day.

But, while his travels provided poignant moments to look back with reverence, Jim also lived in the moment. Wherever he roamed, Jim constantly made friends, and today receives hundreds of Christmas cards every year from friends around the world.

Jim's friends naturally include pilots, especially his World War II 397th Bomb Group, but encompassing a vast network of pilot comrades as well. Pilots share a special bond whether they have flown together or not. Their genuine love of airplanes and their shared experiences of touching the clouds and soaring like eagles give them a natural high reserved for their fraternity.

For more than 25 years, his 397th Bomb Group has met in cities across the country. After my mother passed away, I had the pleasure of attending some of these reunions. At my first one in 1997, my dad and I shared the wonderful experience of Kansas City jazz and the many stories from his fellow wartime buddies. What a wonderful experience. These men have such a unique bond that has remained with them all these years. On the last day, I was touched as they read off the names of those who had died in the past year. Sadly, the group gets smaller every year.

Pilot bonding helped my dad find his way into the cockpit of the Concorde back in 1995. Still young at 74, Dad was enticed by a travel package offered by USAA. Like many military men and women, my dad has always been a big supporter of this major insurance and financial service organization that is dedicated to the military and their dependents. The trip included a flight

Once a pilot, always a pilot.

Lunenburg Town Crier, Nova Scotia.

In the cockpit of the Concorde. D.C. to London, 1993.

from New York to London's Heathrow Airport on the Concorde supersonic jet; flight time: three hours and 20 minutes. Dad would visit London, stay at the five-star Kensington Hotel; travel on the Orient Express from London to Wales; then return to the States via the Queen Elizabeth 2 (QE2). But for "Big Jim," the most memorable event on this excursion was meeting the Flight Captain of the Concorde.

Jim reminisced with a flight attendant about his World War II flying career, and she subsequently relayed his stories to the Concorde's 35-year-old Flight Captain who had served in the British Royal Air Force (RAF). Dad holds a special place in his heart for the RAF pilots who safely escorted many of his WWII missions across the English Channel, and the feeling is mutual. The captain invited Dad into the cockpit. Dad is particularly grateful to have had this special experience on the Concorde, which was retired in 2003.

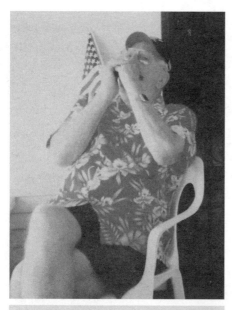

God Bless America.

And always on his travels, Big Jim is ready to entertain with his trusty harmonica at a moment's notice, from annual reunions of his 397th Bomb Group, to joining cruise ships' bands when he travels the high seas. The "Hubba Dubba Man" plays World War II tunes, military medleys, *Take Me Out to the Ball Game*, and, of course, *God Bless America*. It is amazing how this small musical instrument enabled my dad to reach out and touch so many people all his life — and, in return, give him joy as well.

Joining the band.

The "Hubba Dubba Man" at it again!

Jim Sr. & Jr. at PNC Park, Pittsburgh, PA, 2002.

Sharing memories with Joe DeGangi, 1933 NY Yankees Bull Pen Catcher.

THE FAYETTEVILLE OBSERVER   LOCAL & STATE   TUESDAY, JANUARY 29, 2002   3B

Info man leaving courthouse

■ Volunteer Jim Louden has been directing people to the right place for 18 years.

By Missy Stoddard
Staff writer

About two dozen clerks, several dozen boxes of Krispy Kreme doughnuts and a pot of coffee awaited Jim Louden in a break room on the first floor of the Cumberland County Courthouse.

The big man with the healthy head of silver hair chuckled when he saw them. He knew immediately why they had come.

"God bless you, I love you all," he told them. "I'm gonna miss you girls."

For 18 years, the 81-year-old has volunteered his time, which just happens to come with his beaming smile, to sit at the courthouse information booth answering questions and direct

Louden has done under the direction of the Retired Senior Volunteer Program.

Next Monday, he will move into his new home at the Masonic and Eastern Star Retirement Home in Greensboro. Although he is looking forward to the change, he says he leaves Fayetteville with precious memories.

"I've lived here since 1966 and I love the people," he said. "I'm going to the retirement home so my children won't have to worry about me."

For all 18 years, Louden has been joined at the information booth by 87-year-old Carrie Benton. Both have outlived spouses — Benton for 38 years and Louden since 1993, when his wife of 48 years, Peggy, died of brain cancer.

Staff photo by Cindy Burnham

Clerk of Court Linda Priest, left, and Priscilla Person, right, say goodbye to Jim Louden who retired Monday from the Cumberland County Courthouse.

Louden was a natural in the greeter's chair.

"More than anything, he has a look in his eyes and a smile on his face," she said. "It will be hard to replace him."

Korea, Vietnam and in the minican Republic. In Louden was in a devastatin bomber crash at Barksdal Force Base in Louisiana pilot and co-pilot were k but Louden, who was the gator on that flight, surv He spent 2½ years in W Reed Army Hospital recov from injuries such as a b back, arms and legs, a co sion and severe burns. Th he still suffers lingering problems, Louden said he lets it get him down.

"I can still walk," he with pride.

He has traveled extens He couldn't think of a pla the world he has not visite

An avid harmonica pl Louden said that he wishe had his instrument with hi the surprise farewell.

"I would have played

happy smile so much," she said.

Air Force veteran

His job at the courthouse has been easy compared to some of

Honored for volunteer work at Cumberland County Courthouse. Linda Priest & Priscilla Person. —Cindy Burnham; Fayetteville Observer

While he can't play baseball anymore, his passion for the game has continued as a great fan and spectator. Every year, he drives to Florida for baseball spring training and can also be seen in Pittsburgh at PNC Park watching the Pirates play home games.

It has always amazed me that dad constantly travels on planes, trains, and in cars despite his ever-present back pain. Armed with his favorite special cane, he shuffles along until his back needs a rest — then he opens his trusty cane to reveal a little seat. He rests for a moment and then he is on his way once again. As he instructed me, the key to pain management is to get your mind off thinking about the pain and direct it to a better place — enjoyment, fun, helping others, adventure and learning.

Jim's volunteer work increased after he retired, and he received many accolades for his efforts. In 2002, he was voted "Senior Citizen Volunteer of the Year" for working behind the information desk at the Cumberland County Courthouse in Fayetteville.

Giving thanks for his Outstanding NC Senior Citizen Volunteer Award.

In 2003, Jim was voted one of North Carolina's "Most Outstanding Senior Citizens," and that February, Governor Mike Easley paid tribute to him at Trinity Baptist Church in Raleigh. As Jim humbly noted at the ceremony, "To live a great life, you need to be helping others live a great life."

In the past 25 years, Jim has donated more than six gallons of blood to the Cumberland County Blood Assurance Program, in gratitude to all those who provided blood transfusions that saved lives, including his own.

Jim became a Mason in 1954 while stationed in Japan, and with a group of Americans, founded a Masonic Lodge in Nagoya, Torri Masonic Lodge No. 6, which continues to operate in that city today. Upon returning stateside, he transferred his membership to the Creasy Proctor Lodge No. 679 in Fayetteville, NC.

I was always curious about my dad's Masonic commitment, and asked him to tell me about this special organization he has so loved. "Teri," he reflected,

"The Masonic Lodge is a fraternal organization whose members believe in God and hold high ethical and moral ideals. At lodge meetings, we learn and teach what friendship, morality, and truth really mean. What I'm particulary proud of are the programs for charity and relief that I've been able to be a part of over the years. I've always had a special bond with my brothers in the Masons. "

In 2002, Dad surprised my brother and me by announcing that he was moving to Greensboro, North Carolina, after living for 36 years in Fayetteville. Planning ahead for his later years and never once afraid of change, Dad moved into his new home at the Masonic and Eastern Star Retirement Home in Greensboro. It's only fitting that his last earthly home is located on Scottish Rite Court. Dad has always been so proud of his Scottish heritage; the Louden's are descendants of the Campbell clan. Dad has made great friends in Greensboro and loves his Masonic home and his fellowship at the First Lutheran Church.

Once again, he found a new volunteer project. At The Moses H. Cone Memorial Hospital in Greensboro, Jim donates his time as a volunteer for the neurosurgery department. He helps visitors find patients' rooms, provides moral support for patients and their families, and communicates with the physicians and nursing staff. Given the amount of time he spent recuperating at Walter Reed Army Medical Center, Dad understands the challenges patients and families face in a hospital setting.

His Fayetteville Masonic Lodge honored Dad in a special tribute written by its Secretary E. Faison Williams, in 2002.

Helping Others Is a Way of Life for Brother James Leslie Louden.

Creasy Proctor Lodge No. 679 is very fortunate to have among its members many volunteers who support our local community capacities. It is certainly not unusual to find Masons helping out in various avenues within the community. To serve our fellow man in some form is one of our commitments.

I would like to take this opportunity to pay special tribute to one of our members who has spent a tremendous number of hours volunteering his services in many capacities and for many years. He is probably one of the most "unsung" volunteers in our membership. It is an honor and great pleasure to recognize Brother James "Jim" Leslie Louden for his many years of volunteerism.

Brother Jim is a very kind and compassionate individual. He loves life and lives it in a full and Christian way. He is concerned about his friends and fellow Masons and inquires often of their health and needs. He exemplifies the tenets of Masonry in his daily life and is a role model for all of us to follow.

Brother Jim loves life, Masonry, and the friends and Brothers he has come to know over the years. He is easy to meet, easy to love, and if you mind your manners, and ask him nicely, he may just serenade you with a little tune on his harmonica.

He not only gives of his time, but also monetarily. For over 25 years, he has financially supported the Boys & Girls Home at Lake Waccamaw; The Sudan Temple Shriners Hospital Fund for Crippled Children; the Masonic Home for Children in Oxford, North Carolina; and The Masonic & Eastern Star Home for the elderly in Greensboro, North Carolina. He has also supported the Creasy Proctor Lodge yearly fund drives in support of our Masonic Charities.

Brethren, need I say more about the kind heart of Brother James Leslie Louden! What a busy man, serving his fellow man as we should all do. We are fortunate and proud to have Brother Jim as a member of Creasy Proctor Lodge No. 679. Brother Jim attends lodge regularly when not away on some cruise or vacationing in some foreign country. When you see him at lodge again, let him know how much we appreciate his service to our community.

Thanks, Brother Jim, for the donations and time you have devoted to your fellow man. I believe that time is the ultimate gift that one person can give to another. There is a limit to the time we have to share with another person, but we know not how much. Therefore, the time we share comforting or befriending another person is precious. Each minute is priceless! You have given of your time, Brother Jim, in an unselfish manner, which is your nature. I am sure that someday you will hear the Supreme Architect of the Universe say, "Well done, good and faithful servant, enter thou into the joy of thy Lord."

James L. Louden is a 32-degree Scottish Rite Mason and on March 25, 2004 marked his 50th year as a Master Mason.

LOUDEN'S LESSONS

"Reverence and cherish your parents."

— Thomas Jefferson

When Tom Brokaw christened those who came of age during World War II with the name, "The Greatest Generation," he nailed it. This was a generation born in the hey-day of the Roaring '20s, and their folks thought the sky was the limit... until that sky hit them on their heads one dreary day in 1929. And as kids and teenagers, they stood in bread lines, and they knew all too well the song, Brother can you spare a dime?

And no sooner did the depths of The Depression start to lift, did the world begin crumbling all around them... a madman named Adolph was on the loose in Europe, and on a pleasant Sunday morning Japanese bombers paid a call to the tranquil Hawaiian Islands. Suddenly, this generation's young men were ready to give it their all in the fight for freedom, and the young women were ready to rivet the machinery to give them the winning edge.

In some respects, I suppose any generation, including my fellow yuppie peers, would have risen to the occasion, had we been in their shoes at the time. We experienced a bit of that coalescing of a nation after the World Trade Center tragedy on September 11, 2001 when many Americans flew our nation's flag for days, weeks, months.

But we have never really had to walk in anything that resembled this generation's shoes, which, during those Depression years, became resoled with cardboard inlays. Face it, we've had a cushy ride for the past 50 years, and much of the good life we have enjoyed during the years after the Second World War can be traced right back to the sacrifices and spirit of my parents' generation.

As generations pass, it's instructive to see how differently each group viewed the world. There has never been one generation like another. Each has its special times, moments, values, causes, and characteristics.

The key to a progressive civilization is the ability to learn from each previous generation. It is prudent that we examine and learn from our forefathers, incorporating their strengths into our own constitutions and learning from their mistakes as well.

As I write this book in 2004, I am witnessing the passing of my parents' generation. Only one in four World War II veterans is still alive today, and they are leaving us at the rate of more than a thousand per day. And as these veterans leave us, so do their spouses who gave so much of themselves in unheralded ways.

If I have one imperative to pass on to those reading this book, it is to honor and to learn from their parents and their elders; this truly is the key that unlocks the door to self-understanding. We've all heard the platitude, youth is wasted on the young; we've all memorized the fifth of the Ten Commandments, honor thy father and thy mother. But we must appreciate the wisdom of this platitude and follow the commandment.

When I lived at the Coronado Shores high-rise condominium complex, many of my fellow residents were a generation older than me. And I enjoyed the experience immensely. As individuals who had traveled the road of life before me, they had acquired experiences that I had not yet had, and by listening to them, I could reap knowledge, appreciation, and insights. It was a rich experience to tap into these personal histories. And guess what? By tapping into the personal histories of our parents, grandparents, and elders, we each can gain the wisdom that comes from those in advancing years.

I thought I knew my parents, but I actually knew very little until my dad spent time and shared his stories and thoughts with me as I recovered from my injuries.

I thank God that I had the opportunity to really get to know my father, who is still very much alive and active today. And I'm also grateful that I found a way to honor him in a special way, not only with the writing of this book, but also with a monument that will live far beyond his years. He now has a plaque in his honor at the Mount Soledad Veterans War Memorial that stands high on a hill in La Jolla, California, overlooking the Pacific Ocean, beautiful Mission Bay and Downtown San Diego to the south, and the mountains to the east.

The Mount Soledad memorial is one of the most distinctive and unique war memorials in the United States. On this special mountain, Charles Lindbergh once soared in a glider plane, and, during World War II, a radio transmission tower helped fortify our nation's defenses. Veterans, both living and deceased, who served their country during times of war from all branches of military service are honored with individual plaques of black granite. Each plaque contains an etched photograph of the veteran with details of their military service, honors, and family remembrances.

Getting my tribute down to only two lines was no easy task... but it was a hit with "Big Jim"!

64 combat Missions with the "Bridge Busters"
and "God as his first Pilot."

"Big Jim's" moral-building harmonica tunes
earned him the nickname "Hubba Dubba Man."

My special tribute to Dad, Mt. Soledad War Memorial, La Jolla, CA.

Honoring our veterans. Never Forget. Mt. Soledad War Memorial, La Jolla, CA.

The Louden Family: Les, Jim Jr., & Teri with "Big Jim" playing "God Bless America."

At Mount Soledad, I've seen veterans get teary-eyed, choked up, and unable to speak when family members have unveiled a plaque to let them know they have the gratitude not only of their family but also of a grateful nation. And it happened big time when "Big Jim" was surprised with his own plaque.

We unveiled Dad's plaque on July 5, 2003. Friends and family were in town to celebrate my 50th birthday, and Dad thought we were on our way to my birthday party. As a matter of fact, we were, but unbeknownst to Dad, I had pre-arranged for 40 of us to meet at the memorial. As we headed up the mountain, I said, "Hey, Dad, we've got a few minutes; let me show you this beautiful war memorial."

Friends and family greeted Dad upon our arrival, including my brother and my nephew, and representatives of the Mount Soledad Memorial

Association. In a formal ceremony arranged in conjunction with the Association's Board of Trustees, we unveiled Dad's plaque, and, like so many other veterans honored on the mountaintop, Dad became overwhelmed with emotion. He was speechless... and Dad is never speechless.

I gave a short speech to acquaint all the attendees with his "miracle life" and many accomplishments; an American flag was raised, lowered, properly folded, and presented to Dad. And we sang God Bless America, accompanied, of course, by "Big Jim," the "Hubba Dubba Man" on his harmonica.

Dad's plaque is mounted on the west side of Wall "F," just steps away from a plaque honoring Major Alton Glenn Miller, placed there by his daughter, Jonnie. Some sixty years ago, Dad waited for Glenn Miller to lead the Army Air Corps Band in Paris, and although that was never to be, now they have connected. And Dad is also once again in the company of Bob Hope who entertained him and his fellow servicemen in Turkey; Hope's plaque was dedicated on Veterans Day 2003, placed on the mountain by two of his children, Linda and Kelly. It's just a few plaques to the right of my dad's.

I wouldn't be surprised if 50 years from now, a visitor up on that mountain swears he hears the faint sounds of a trombone, a harmonica, and a voice singing a familiar tune...

"Thanks For The Memories."

I learned so much from my dad on my journey to write this book. It's not a stretch to say that he rescued me in my deepest pain and restored my soul. During my childhood, our household was grounded in the Lord God above and our faith in Jesus Christ. But, alas, like so many of my peers on the fast track, I became too busy and preoccupied, climbing higher and higher up that corporate ladder. As I began to exercise more "control" over my corporate empire, I forgot who was really in control. Years later, Dad reminded me... gently, patiently, God has always been his first pilot. And

"Like father, like daughter."

now, my faith is once again strong and solid. Not surprisingly, so is my healed body, my circle of friends, and, well… everything.

Dad's upbeat philosophy of life and living is filled with positive and optimistic expressions. You wouldn't always recognize them as "spiritual," but if you think about them a bit, you'll see that they surely are.

I call them "Louden's Lessons." I often turn to them for a little pick-me-up. I hope you will refer to a few of them often and that they give you inspiration and bring a smile to your face.

ℒOUDEN'S LESSONS

On Feelin' Good:
"Make other people feel good and you'll feel better yourself;
remember names and you'll never meet a stranger."

On Miracles:
"Believe in them; they happen every day."

On Worries:
"Let God be your First Pilot and leave your worries behind."

On Today:
"Yesterday's a cancelled check, tomorrow is a promissory note, and
every day begins a new chapter."

On Pain:
"You can take your mind off pain by helping others, relaxing,
meditating, and never feeling sorry for yourself."

On America:
"Be grateful you are an American every day; God bless America,
and thank all those men and women who give of themselves
to keep our nation free."

On Wants:
"Pray for blessings, not things. Be satisfied and grateful
for what you have, and remember, there are always those
who have less."

On Friends:
"Friends are quiet angels who lift us to our feet
when our wings have trouble remembering how to fly."

On Parenting:
"Give your children roots, but also give them wings."

On Work:
"If you think you're working, you're in the wrong job.
Find your passion."

On Havin' Fun:
"Make it a goal to have fun; laugh and never lose your smile."

On Adventure:
"Spread your wings to catch more life."

On Stress:
"Slow down; smell those roses."

On Fear:
"Fear is different than being afraid. Fear keeps you on your toes,
while being afraid makes you nervous. There are old pilots, and
there are bold pilots. But there are no old, bold pilots."

On Birthdays:
"Celebrate the miracle of every one. Love them while they last."

On Flying:
"Wish for blue skies, fair winds... and great mechanics."

And, of course, On Living:
"Ask, and it shall be given you; Seek, and ye shall find;
Knock, and it shall be opened unto you." – Matthew 7:7

*Dad, thanks for sharing your memories and lessons.
God bless each and every one of you,
and here's to a wonderful life on God's wings.*

SOURCES CITED

B-26 Martin Marauders of the 397th Bomb Group (M), Open Edition
Artist-Signed Print, *The Aviation Art of Randy Green*;
www.randygreenart.com.

Knaak, Marcelle Size. *Encyclopedia of U.S. Air Force Aircraft and Missile Systems,
Volume II, Post-World War II Bombers.*1945-1973.

Department of Veterans Affairs, Regional Office, 251 North Main St.,
Winston-Salem, NC.

Noel Memorial Library, Archives and Special Collections, One University Place,
Shreveport, Louisiana 71115; Shreveport Times Collection and
Jack Barham Collection, Noel Memorial Library Archives,
Louisiana State University in Shreveport.

NA XB-45 Tornado general briefing data, *Aeroplane Monthly*,
October 1987, pp 511-513.

The Shreveport Journal, Shreveport, LA

"*A Life Full of Adventure is his to live*," Article ID 324199, Larry Cheek,
The Fayetteville Observer. Jan. 14, 2000.

"*Jim Louden's Creed is living For Today*," Article ID 427051, Larry Cheek, The
Fayetteville Observer. Sept. 20, 1995.

"*The Shirt Off His Back*," Article ID 610004, Larry Cheek,
The Fayetteville Observer. May 13, 1988.

"*The T-Shirt*," *The Legacy of the Daedalus – War Stories and Flying Tales*,
pp 180-182, Larry Cheek; Daedalian Foundation, PO Box 249,
Randolph AFB, Texas 78148.

Department of the Air Force, Air Force Historical Research Agency,
Maxwell Air Force Base, Alabama.

Unites States Air Force Museum, Wright-Patterson AFB, Dayton, Ohio.

Reichelt Program for Oral History, Florida State University, Florida 32306-2200.

History of Flight, North American Aviation, U.S. Centennial of Flight
Commission, www.centennialofflight.gov.

The ON GOD'S WINGS CD

Join Teri as she interviews her dad throughout this heart-warming and educational journey. Big Jim, The "Hubba Dubba Man," has been entertaining people all over the world with his trusty harmonica and storytelling for more than half a century.

Now, you can hear him for yourself. Recorded at Audio Productions in Nashville, Tennessee in May 2004, this CD will stir memories and bring a smile to your face.

Teri and "Big Jim" havin' a fun time on recording day in Music City USA!

THE STORIES

Laugh and smile as you listen to Jim recounting his touching portrayal of past adventures and how to live a great life.

✯ Tales from "The Greatest Generation"

✯ Trying out for Major League Baseball

✯ D-Day & The Battle of the Bulge

✯ His miracle survival story

✯ Love of flying, family, military, God, and country

THE MUSIC

Get ready to tap your toes and sing to this
great collection of tunes including:

✯ "Take Me Out to the Ballgame"

✯ "God Bless America"

✯ "The official Air Force,
Navy, Marine and
Army songs"

✯ "The White Cliffs
of Dover"

✯ "Amazing Grace"

✯ And many more...

*Jim Gilmore and Colin Parker from Audio Productions
& "Big Jim" with his accompanist, guitarist Rip Williams*

*"It's a wonderful and amazing treat to hear Big Jim recount his stories.
What an inspiration. The "Hubba Dubba Man" doesn't take anything for granted.
He lives every day to the fullest."*

–Gregory Page, Singer-Songwriter, San Diego, CA

*"Playing my guitar along with Big Jim on his harmonica is one of my fondest
memories. His passion for harmonica playing and entertaining others is evident,
along with his spiritual gifts and infectious passion for life."*

–Rip Williams, Musician, Nashville, TN

To order, log onto our website at
www.ongodswings.com
or call 800-214-6811

Shreveport Jo

2 DIE IN JET BOMI

Third Man
Seriously
Injured

Accident Occu
Within Sight Of

Two men w
and a third se
jured about l
Thursday whe
four-engined je
attached to
seventh bomb
Barksdale Air

RIDAY, JUNE 10, 1949

ttsburgher Hurt
Jet Plane Crash

Brentwood War Ace
s Lone Survivor

Pittsburgh air hero was in ical condition today after the sh of a jet bomber near ksdale Field, La.

apt. James L. Louden, 28, of W. Garden Rd., Brentwood, the only survivor after a bomber plunged into a hill in a landing approach. The engine bomber, capable of ds up to 500 miles an hour, st into flames immediately.

'Bridge Buster' Group

apt. Louden served as a flight mander with a B-26 "Bridge ter" group in World War II. was awarded the Distinged Flying Cross for leading flight through heavy enemy osition to carry out assignts during the Normandy inon.

e left the University of Pittsh to enter the Air Corps completed more than 60 miss in Europe.

outine Training Operation

sterday's flight was a routraining operation to test the bombers, one of the world's st.

led instantly in the crash Capt. Ralph L. Smith of veport, La., and Capt. Milton

CAPT. JAMES L. LOUDEN
Pittsburgher hurt in crash.

Crash Victim
Still Critical

Capt. James L. Lou cally injured in a B-45 jet bor crash here last Thursday, wa ported "improved" last night the public information office Barksdale Air Force base.

Although the Captain recogn his wife, who came here f Pittsburgh, Pa., Barksdale aut ties said his condition could be termed as critical. He has in a coma since the time of the cident and has regained consc ness only for brief intervals.

Captain Louden, whose hom in Pittsburgh, is public relat officer for the 47th bombardn wing at Barksdale, the first op tional training unit of B-45's in nation.

A seven-man military bo which is investigating the p crash which took the lives of other Air Force officers is sc uled to deliver a report early week.